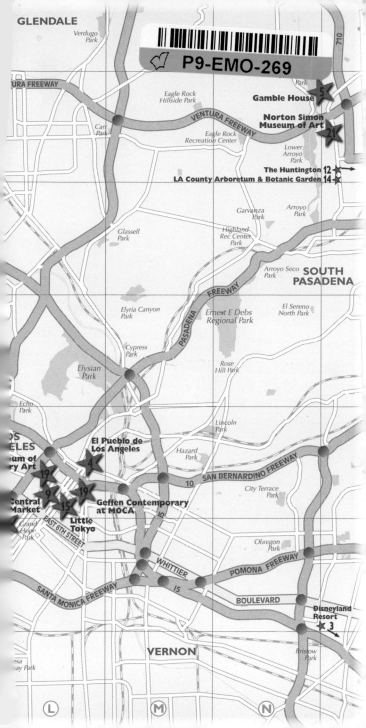

GLENDALE

Verdugo Park

P9-EMO-269

VENTURA FREEWAY

Eagle Rock Hillside Park

Park

Gamble House 5

VENTURA FREEWAY

Carr Park

Eagle Rock Recreation Center

Norton Simon Museum of Art 21

Lower Arroyo Park

The Huntington 12 →
LA County Arboretum & Botanic Garden 14 →

Garvanza Park

Arroyo Park

Glassell Park

Highland Rec Center Park

Arroyo Seco Park

SOUTH PASADENA

Elyria Canyon Park

Ernest E Debs Regional Park

El Sereno North Park

PASADENA FREEWAY

Cypress Park

Rose Hill Park

Elysian Park

Echo Park

Lincoln Park

LOS ANGELES

...um of ...ry Art

El Pueblo de Los Angeles 4

Hazard Park

19

19

9

Geffen Contemporary at MOCA

...Central Market

15

Little Tokyo

Grand Hope Park

EAST 6TH STREET

SAN BERNARDINO FREEWAY

10

City Terrace Park

I5

Obregon Park

WHITTIER

POMONA FREEWAY

SANTA MONICA FREEWAY

15

BOULEVARD

Disneyland Resort 3 →

...sa ...way Park

VERNON

Bristow Park

Ⓛ   Ⓜ   Ⓝ

Fodor's 25BEST
Los Angeles

by Emma Stanford

Fodor's Travel Publications
New York • Toronto • London • Sydney • Auckland
www.fodors.com

Contents

KEY TO SYMBOLS

- 🆔 Map reference to the accompanying pull-out map
- ✉ Address
- ☎ Telephone number
- 🕐 Opening/closing times

- 🍴 Restaurant or café
- 🚃 Nearest rail station
- 🚌 Nearest bus route
- ⛴ Nearest riverboat or ferry stop
- ✈ Nearest airport

ENTERTAINMENT 124

Whether you're after a cultural fix or just want a place to relax with a drink after a hard day's sightseeing, we've made the best choices for you.

EAT 138

Uncover great dining experiences, from a quick bite at lunch to top-notch evening meals.

SLEEP 150

We've brought together the best hotels in the city, whatever budget you're on.

NEED TO KNOW 160

The practical information you need to make your trip run smoothly.

PULL-OUT MAP

The pull-out map accompanying this book is a comprehensive street plan of the city. We've given grid references within the book for each sight and listing.

🦽 Facilities for visitors with disabilities
ℹ️ Tourist information
❓ Other practical information

📖 Admission charges: Expensive (over $15), Moderate ($6–$15) and Inexpensive (under $6)
▷ Further information

3

Introducing Los Angeles

Squeezed into 4,752sq miles (12,308sq km), split by a mountain range and flanked by the Pacific Ocean, this megalopolis of more than 10 million people has been made famous by novels, movies, TV shows and—despite the smog—sunny weather.

Los Angeles is a magnet for immigrants, becoming in many respects the northernmost Latin American city and the easternmost Asian city. It is a tremendous draw for tourists, with over 25 million overnight visitors arriving each year.

Sprawling LA is often described as lacking an urban core, which is tough to dispute: Visitors can't take in LA County by exploring just a few square miles. Time and energy are required, but the region rewards anyone who is willing to expend a bit of both.

Few cities match the enticements showcased here: gorgeous beaches, theme parks, world-class museums and theater, and glitzy celebrities and fashions. The city is as disparate and complex as the many writers who set their stories here, from Raymond Chandler and Robert Towne to Joan Didion and Walter Mosely.

For a visitor, this means that a trip to LA is a collection of experiences, each with a different feel and backstory. And the story is constantly changing, as many neighborhoods are enjoying resurgences, from back-to-its-glam-roots Hollywood to Culver City, with its celebrity chefs, art galleries and increasingly bustling nightlife. And other neighborhoods such as Santa Monica, Venice and Beverly Hills remain as popular and well visited as ever. From West LA's glitzy shopping promenades and less-touristy neighborhoods like Los Feliz, to the sun-kissed shorelines and soaring coastal mountains, you'll always find more to explore.

With all there is to do and see, including dining in hip restaurants, browsing in stylish stores and viewing priceless artwork, it's hard to slow down and let yourself slip into the southern California rhythm. But one thing is for sure, when you do, LA, with its laid-back ways (except in heavy traffic), will get under your skin, even if that skin isn't taut and tanned!

FACTS AND FIGURES

● LA has the tallest building between Chicago and Taipei, the 1,018ft (310m) US Bank Tower.
● LA is home to nine Frank Lloyd Wright structures and a dozen or so by Frank Gehry, including the Hollywood Bowl.
● LA has the fourth-largest economy in the US.

DEARLY DEPARTED

LA is home to plenty of celebrities—some dearly departed. Luminaries like Truman Capote, Merv Griffin and Jayne Mansfield have graves or memorials at LA cemeteries. For many years Joe DiMaggio made sure the most famous crypt—of his ex-wife, Marilyn Monroe—was adorned with flowers several times a week.

WHAT'S IN A NAME?

Street and neighborhood names in Los Angeles are as varied as the city. Venice, with its canals and boardwalk, is a tribute to the Italian city, while Century City's moniker comes from the movie studio, 20th Century Fox. And busy Pico Boulevard was named for Pio Pico, the last governor of Mexican "Alta" California.

NICKNAMES

Nicknames abound for Los Angeles, including the obvious LA, along with La-la-Land, the Southland, the City of Angels, Lotusville and El Pueblo ("the town" in Spanish). Folks from Hollywood might be called Hollywoodites, Hollywoodians or Hollywooders. Anyone from Long Beach is simply a Long Beacher.

Focus On Architecture

Better known as a pop-culture capital, LA, surprisingly, is a haven for the arts, with top museums and a dynamic gallery scene drawing contemporary artists from around the globe. Prize-winning architects from California and abroad have found creative space to innovate new buildings here.

Arts and Crafts

In the early 1900s, the Arts and Crafts style of architecture became Southern California's paradigm. Harmony with nature and interior designs that were carved, painted and sculpted by hand were the guiding principles of renowned architects Greene & Greene. The Greene brothers designed many exemplary Arts and Crafts bungalows in suburban Pasadena, including the Gamble House (▷ 22–23) that was influenced by Japanese arts and architectural traditions. Likewise, Frank Lloyd Wright merged indoor and outdoor living spaces at the Hollyhock House (▷ 14–15), with its pre-Columbian design motifs.

Depression-era Deco

After the stock market crashed in 1929, the Great Depression took hold of the country. Yet in LA, the 1930s saw a building boom of art- deco movie houses and skyscrapers, often financed by Hollywood and oil industry wealth. Some art-deco gems are still standing Downtown, along Mid-City's "Miracle Mile," in Hollywood and in Santa Monica by the beach. Many of Downtown's art-deco masterpieces— including the Oviatt Building (▷ 70) and the Broadway Historic Theatre District (▷ 66)— can be visited on guided walking tours given by the LA Conservancy (tel 213/430-4219; www.laconservancy.org).

The World Moves In

Both during and after World War II, LA's population exploded as Americans migrated to

Clockwise from top: Tramway Gas Station, now Palm Springs Visitor Center; a wooden staircase at the Gamble House; Hollyhock House by Frank Lloyd Wright;

Southern California looking for work and a fresh start. Some artistic and intellectual expatriates from Europe and beyond did the same. Although New York City was then the center of the USA's avant-garde scene, many painters exhibited works in Los Angeles and were inspired by Southern California landscapes. This was despite LA's city council declaring modern art to be Communist propaganda and forbidding its public display beginning in 1951, a mandate largely ignored.

Modernism

In the 1960s, Southern California architecture came to be defined by modernism. Visionary European architects such as Richard Neutra and Rudolph Schindler had been in LA since the late 1920s, but it wasn't until mid-century that the modernist style reached its zenith. Modernism's clean lines and soaring glass walls were influenced by Europe's International and Bauhaus styles, but imbued with more organic shapes.

Pop to Post-Modern

The 1960s, 1970s and 1980s were a fertile time for the visual arts in LA, especially for pop artists such as Venice Beach's Edward Ruscha. Newly founded art museums and galleries mounted groundbreaking exhibits at the Los Angeles County Museum of Art (▷ 46–47) and Museum of Contemporary Art (▷ 50–51). The first full retrospective of Marcel Duchamp's work was a watershed event for Pasadena in 1963. In the 1990s, Santa Monica's Bergamot Station (▷ 115), and West LA's showpiece Getty Center (▷ 24–25), known for its distinctive postmodern architectural design by Richard Meier, opened. No contemporary LA architect is as widely recognized as Frank Gehry, whose sculptural forms appear to defy gravity, like at Downtown's Walt Disney Concert Hall (Music Center, ▷ 134).

architectural detail of the entrance hall to the Getty Center; the grand staircase to the Kodak Theatre; the art-deco lobby entrance of the Oviatt Building

Top Tips For...

These great suggestions will help you tailor your ideal visit to Los Angeles, no matter how you choose to spend your time.

...Designer Labels
Visit Fred Segal in **Santa Monica** (▷ 117) and on **Melrose Avenue** (▷ 48–49).
Head to **Montana Avenue** (▷ 120) in Santa Monica for boutique shopping.
Meander along **Rodeo Drive** (▷ 121) for the high-end retail experience.

...Funky and Unusual Finds
Try on vintage clothes at **Wasteland** (▷ 123).
Visit **Chung King Road** (▷ 116), Downtown.
Check out antiques on **Abbot Kinney Boulevard** (▷ 115).
Pop into a gallery in Santa Monica's **Bergamot Station** (▷ 115).

...A Hearty Meal in the Morning
Fill up at **Kokomo** (▷ 145).
Nibble at **La Brea Bakery** (▷ 145).
Dine Downtown at ex-mayor Riordan's **Original Pantry Café** (▷ 147).
Splurge on a hotel brunch at **Shutters on the Beach** (▷ 159).

...Distinct Architecture
See a show at Frank Gehry's **Walt Disney Concert Hall** (Music Center, ▷ 134).
Stroll around the grounds of the **Getty Center** (▷ 24–25).
Tour **Hollyhock House** (▷ 14–15), LA's most famous Frank Lloyd Wright structure.

...Fun in the Sun
Visit the **LA County Arboretum & Botanic Garden** (▷ 40–41).
Hop on a trolley tour of **Beverly Hills** (▷ 17).
Learn to surf at **Aqua Surf School** (▷ 129).
Take a gondola ride in Long Beach after a visit to the *Queen Mary* (▷ 44–45).

Clockwise from top: Dazzling flower baskets enhance a shopping trip to Rodeo Drive; reach for the stars on Hollywood Walk of Fame; the famous Ferris wheel on

…A Night Out
See an old film at the **Silent Movie Theatre** (▷ 135–136).
Traverse the universe at a show in **Griffith Observatory's** planetarium (▷ 32–33).
Hear live music at **McCabe's Guitar Shop** (▷ 133).

…Saving Your Pennies
Ride the bus to the free-admission **Getty Center** (▷ 24–25).
Saunter down **Hollywood Boulevard** and the Walk of Fame (▷ 34–35).
Hike in **Topanga Canyon** (▷ 72).
Rest your head at the friendly, inexpensive **Farmer's Daughter** (▷ 156).

…Living the High Life
Enjoy a massage at **Thibiant Beverly Hills** (▷ 136) or **Burke Williams Day Spa** (▷ 130).
Have tea and rub shoulders with celebs at the **Peninsula Beverly Hills** (▷ 159).
Place a bet on the horses at **Santa Anita Race Track** (▷ 135).
Dine in elegant surroundings at **Patina** (▷ 147–148) or **Valentino** (▷ 149).

…Your Kids
Ride the Ferris wheel at the **Santa Monica Pier** (▷ 56).
Spend time with Mickey and friends at **Disneyland Resort** (▷ 18–19).
Entertain the family at **Universal Studios** (▷ 60–61) and **Knott's Berry Farm** (▷ 73).
See skeletons and fossilized remains at **La Brea Tar Pits and Page Museum** (▷ 38–39).

…Celeb Spotting
Relax with celebrities at **The Ivy** on Robertson Boulevard (▷ 144).
Shop on **Montana Avenue** (▷ 120).
Reserve a spot on the **Warner Brothers Studio VIP tour** (▷ 72).

Santa Monica Pier; Queen Mary moored at Long Beach; tropical foliage, a highlight of the LA County Arboretum & Botanic Garden; Getty Center

Timeline

1818 The Avila Adobe house, LA's oldest dwelling, is built for cattle rancher and mayor Don Francisco Avila.

1821 California becomes a territory of Mexico.

BEGINNINGS

The Indian village of Yang-Na stood near Los Angeles River, close to the present-day site of City Hall. In 1771 Father Junípèro Serra and Gaspar de Portolá discovered the village and within months, Mission San Gabriel Arcángel was founded. Ten years later Los Pobladores, 44 farmer-settlers from Mexico, reached the San Gabriel mission and established El Pueblo de Nuestra Señora la Reina de los Angeles in the fertile Los Angeles basin.

TINSELTOWN

Hollywood and the film industry employed more people in Los Angeles than any other industry in the 1940s. In 1974, the Owens Valley Water Wars (a dispute between LA and the Owens Valley) were fictionalized in the film *Chinatown*.

1842 Gold is discovered in the San Fernando Valley, six years before the discovery at Sutter's Mill that triggered the Gold Rush.

1848 End of Mexican-American War. California becomes part of the US.

1876 The first transcontinental railway (Southern Pacific) arrives in LA.

1880 The University of Southern California is founded.

1881 Captain Harrison Gray Otis launches the *Los Angeles Times*.

1892 Oil is discovered Downtown.

1902 Los Angeles' first movie house, the Tally's Electric Theatre, opens on Main Street. First Rose Bowl college football game held.

1909 Santa Monica Pier opens.

1911 The Nestor Motion Picture Co. founds Hollywood's first movie

The sun goes down on the Ferris wheel, a historic landmark on Santa Monica Pier

Join the Gold Rush at Sutter's Mill

studio in the Blondeau Tavern at Sunset and Gower.

1919 The United Artists Film Corporation is founded by D. W. Griffith, Mary Pickford, Douglas Fairbanks and Charlie Chaplin to improve actors' pay and working conditions.

1927 The Academy of Motion Picture Arts and Sciences hosts its first awards ceremony.

1932 The Olympic Games comes to LA. They will return in 1984.

1955 Disneyland opens.

1965 Riots in Watts rage for six days, leaving 34 dead and 1,032 wounded

1992 Riots follow the acquittal of four white police officers accused of beating African American motorist Rodney King.

2003 Designed by Frank Gehry, the $240 million Walt Disney Concert Hall opens, helping to revitalize Downtown.

2010 The LA Lakers basketball team beat their archrivals Boston Celtics to win the NBA championships at Downtown's Staples Center.

WATER

As LA boomed around 1900, the demand for water became a major issue. When water bureau superintendent William Mulholland suggested an aqueduct to transport melted snow from the Sierra Nevada to feed the growing city, he was thought to be mad. However, the aqueduct, all 223 miles (359km) and 142 tunnels of it, opened in 1913, and with a 105-mile (169km) extension into the Mono Basin, still serves the city.

NATURAL DISASTERS

In 1993 Malibu witnessed the worse bush fires in their history, causing $200 million of damage. In 1994 an earthquake (6.8 on the Richter scale) killed 55 and did $20 billion of damage.

Los Angeles burning during the 1992 riots

Academy Awards trophies, a Hollywood symbol

Top 25

This section contains the must-see Top 25 sights and experiences in Los Angeles. They are listed alphabetically, and numbered so you can locate them on the inside front cover map.

TOP 25

★ 1 Barnsdall Art Park and Hollyhock House

HIGHLIGHTS

- Hollyhock House interior
- Views over Hollywood from Barnsdall Art Park
- Free summer Shakespeare performances

LA's architectural treasure was designed by Frank Lloyd Wright. Visitors can explore the bold lines of Hollyhock House and view local artists' work in the gallery on the grounds.

Hollyhock House When unconventional millionaire oil heiress Aline Barnsdall arrived in Los Angeles in 1915 from Chicago she intended to found a theatrical community. She bought a 36-acre (15ha) site called Olive Hill, on the eastern side of Hollywood, and commissioned architect Frank Lloyd Wright to design the project. The full plan was never realized because of artistic and financial differences, but the residence was completed in 1921. The concrete-and-stucco building, which has a square shape reminiscent of pre-Columbian

Left: The Living Room in Hollyhock House—named after the flower, hollyhocks are found on the roofline, walls, columns and furnishings; below: Hollyhock House, Frank Lloyd Wrights first building styled on pre-Columbian architecture

architecture, was named Hollyhock House after Aline Barnsdall's favorite flower, and stylized hollyhocks decorate the building inside and out.

Neglect and renovation Barnsdall gave the property to the city in 1927 for use as a public art park. It was altered over the years as different tenants used it, and earthquakes and weather also took their toll. It was designated a city monument in 1963, but only in 2000 was it shut down for a thorough restoration.

Art park The grounds officially reopened as Barnsdall Art Park in 2003. It contains the Los Angeles Municipal Art Gallery, which displays works by local and international artists, and the Barnsdall Gallery Theatre, where local groups stage performances.

THE BASICS

www.hollyhockhouse.net
www.barnsdallartpark.com

➕ K5

✉ Barnsdall Art Park, 4800 Hollywood Boulevard, Los Feliz

☎ 323/644-6269

🕐 Tours Wed–Sun 12.30, 1.30, 2.30, 3.30 (reservations required for groups of 10 or more)

🚇 Metro Red Line

🚌 DASH Hollywood, Los Feliz

♿ Moderate

HIGHLIGHTS

● People-watching in the Golden Triangle
● Brunch or a cocktail at a luxury hotel
● Shopping for haute couture on Rodeo Drive

You can't say you've "done LA" until you've seen Beverly Hills. The city's most recognizable ZIP code (90210) is also LA's most visited neighborhood, receiving over five million visitors a year.

A star is born In a classic rags-to-riches story, the countrified suburb of Beverly Hills, west of Hollywood, was plucked from obscurity by movie stars—Douglas Fairbanks Jr. set up home here in 1919, followed by Charlie Chaplin, Gloria Swanson and Rudolph Valentino; and so it began.

Seeing the sights Historical Beverly Hills walking tour maps are available from the Visitors Bureau. The walk takes about two hours and covers such local sights as the imposing

Clockwise from far left: O'Neill House at 507 N. Rodeo Drive; shoppers indulge at Tiffany & Co., Rodeo Drive; Tudor-style Greystone Mansion, not what you would expect to find in Beverly Hills; the art-deco, retro-style Beverly Hills Civic Center; street signs point the way to the best retail therapy

City Hall, Beverly Gardens and the wonderful Gaudí-like O'Neill House at No. 507 N. Rodeo Drive, or gawk at all of the art, architecture and historical landmarks on a narrated trolley tour. If you want to see movie moguls at play, try the Polo Lounge at the flamingo-pink Beverly Hills Hotel (▷ 154–155). To watch a television program or listen to a radio show from the 1920s to the present day, visit the Paley Center for Media (▷ 71).

Wide-open spaces With so many gorgeous mansions in the area, it's no surprise that Beverly Hills is also home to exquisite gardens. The estate of Virginia Robinson (tours by appointment only, ▷ 72), which is on the National Register of Historic Places, features tropical flowers and plants.

THE BASICS

✚ F5–F6

Beverly Hills Conference & Visitors Bureau
www.beverlyhillsbchere. com
✉ 239 S. Beverly Drive, Beverly Hills
☎ 310/248-1015; 800/345-2210
🕐 Mon–Fri 8.30–5
🚌 14, 20, 270

Beverly Hills Trolley Tour
✉ Rodeo Drive/Dayton Way
☎ 310/285-2442
🕐 Year-round tours Sat–Sun; extended hours in Jul–Aug, Dec (trolleys do not operate in the rain). Tour duration 40 min
🎫 Moderate

3 Disneyland Resort

© Disney

© Disney

HIGHLIGHTS

● World of Color show
(DCA's Paradise Pier)
● Space Mountain
(Tomorrowland)
● California Screamin'
(DCA's Paradise Pier)
● Pirates of the Caribbean
(New Orleans Square)
● Splash Mountain (Critter
Country)
● Soarin' Over California
(DCA's Golden State)

TIP

● Save money and time
by buying your tickets in
advance online.

Since Disneyland opened its doors in
1955, Disney theme parks have become
a worldwide phenomenon. The 80-acre
(32ha) park, with its beguiling shows and
attractions, is still the daddy of them all.

Magic Kingdom Brilliantly conceived and
operated like Swiss clockwork, the self-
proclaimed "Happiest Place on Earth" remains
a perennial winner. Disney's particular brand
of fantasy appeals across almost all age and
cultural barriers. The park is divided into eight
individually themed "lands." The gates open
onto Main Street, U.S.A., a pastiche Victorian
street lined with shops, which leads to the hub
of the park at Sleeping Beauty Castle. From
here you can explore the tropically inspired
Adventureland, home to the rattling roller

From far left: Visitors prepare for an exciting day out at the Magic Kingdom; expect to get wet at Splash Mountain; a Disney spectacle of light reflecting onto the lake

© Disney

coaster ride Indiana Jones™ Adventure, or take a turn around Wild West-style Frontierland. Small children favor the simpler, cartoon-like rides in Fantasyland and Mickey's Toontown, while New Orleans Square is occupied by the spooky Haunted Mansion. Tomorrowland is a vision of the future. Disney California Adventure, an adjacent 58-acre (23ha) park, pays homage to the Golden State's unique character. Highlights, in five distinct areas, include a carnival pier, movie studio backlot and Route 66-themed Cars Land.

Think ahead From July to early September, and during holidays year-round, the parks are very crowded and lines can be long. At select rides, the free FASTPASS system saves your place in line, shortening wait times.

THE BASICS

www.disneyland.com
🔒 Off map, southeast
✉ 1313 S. Harbor Boulevard (off I–5/Santa Ana Freeway), Anaheim
☎ 714/781-4565
🕐 Daily. Hours vary; approximate times peak 8am–midnight, low 10–8
🍴 Snack bars, cafés and restaurants
🚌 460; ART shuttles Amtrak, Metrolink Orange County Line
♿ Excellent
💲 Expensive

HIGHLIGHTS

● Authentic, first-rate Mexican food
● *La América Tropical*, a mural by Mexican artist David Siqueiros
● *Día De Los Muertos* (Day of the Dead) festivities on November 1

Angelenos tend to be snooty about the touristy Olvera Street market, but Sunday's mariachi masses in the Old Plaza Church are worthwhile, as are the more conventional historic sights.

LA's historic heart The site of the original 1781 pueblo settlement covers just a few blocks, yet within its confines are many historic buildings and sites, including museums, restaurants, stores and a Mexican market. The main thoroughfare is pedestrianized Olvera Street, leading off La Placita, the former town plaza shaded by Moreton Bay fig trees. On the south side of the plaza is the original 1884 Firehouse No. 1, which displays antique firefighting equipment. To the west is the city's oldest Catholic church, near La Plaza de Cultura

Clockwise from far left: Mural by Leo Politi on the Biscailuz Building on Campo Santo; a room inside Avila Adobe, LA's oldest adobe; sombreros for sale on a stall at Olvera Street market; the 1884 El Pueblo firehouse

y Artes, which offers Mexican American art and history exhibits and live performances.

Sterling support Olvera Street fell into disrepair around the turn of the 19th century when the downtown area moved south. By 1926, it was a grimy alley until local civic leader Christine Sterling stepped in. Her campaign to rescue the historic buildings and inaugurate the market is exhibited at the restored Avila Adobe.

Mexican marketplace Across the street, the Visitor Center in the 1887 Sepulveda House distributes walking tour maps and shows a short historical video. The daily market is still going strong, and the crowded thoroughfare is bursting with stalls selling everything from Mexican pottery and leatherware to sombreros.

THE BASICS

www.elpucblo.lacity.org
www.olvera-street.com

Visitor Center

✚ L6

✉ 622 N. Main Street

☎ 213/628-1274

🕐 Daily 9–4. Olvera Street: daily 10 8. Closed national hols

🚌 DASH B, D

🚉 Union Station

♿ Few

🎫 Free

❓ Walking tours Tue–Sat at 10, 11 and 12 (meet next to firehouse)

Museums

🕐 Avila Adobe: daily 9–4. Firehouse and Chinese American: Tue–Sun 10–3

🎫 Free

HIGHLIGHTS

- Front entrance: leaded glass by Emil Lange
- Main staircase
- Sitting room: carved reliefs of birds and plants
- Rugs from Greene and Greene designs
- Guest bedroom: maple furnishings inlaid with silver

TIP

- Tour tickets may sell out, so arrive early; reservations are accepted only for the Thu–Sun 2pm tour.

The Gamble House takes the utilitarian California Bungalow and turns it into an art form: Every impeccably handcrafted inch of the house is a masterpiece.

California Bungalow The Gamble House, designed by brothers Charles and Henry Greene for David and Mary Gamble (of Procter and Gamble fame), is the most well-preserved example of luxurious wooden "bungalows" built in the early 20th century. The informal bungalow-style residence represented an appealing escape from Victorian stuffiness, and it was swiftly translated into southern California's architectural vernacular.

A symphony in wood However, it's far from a traditional bungalow. Greene and Greene's

Clockwise from far left: The dining room, main staircase and living room are perfect examples of the beautifully handcrafted wood displayed inside; the wooden exterior is just as impressive; wood and lantern detail in the living room

spreading two-floor design, with its Swiss- and Japanese-influenced lines, was planned in meticulous detail. The site was chosen to catch cool breezes from the arroyo, and the arrangement of spacious verandas shaded by upper-floor sleeping porches and overhanging eaves keeps the house comfortably ventilated. Working largely in wood, the Greenes cloaked the exterior with shingles and created a rich, golden-timbered interior. Every fixture and fitting, from the dining room furniture to the irons in the fireplace, was custom-built, and many of the schemes were designed to complement Mary Gamble's favorite possessions, such as Tiffany table lamps and opalescent Rookwood pottery. The excellent bookstore also sells self-guiding tour maps of other historic homes within the vicinity.

THE BASICS

www.gamblehouse.org

🏠 P3

✉ 4 Westmoreland Place, Pasadena (off N. Orange Grove Boulevard)

☎ 626/793-3334

🕐 Thu–Sun 12–4 (last ticket sold at 3). Closed national hols

🚌 267

♿ None

💲 Moderate

❓ Admission by guided tour only, duration 1 hour; frequent departures

HIGHLIGHTS

- Ludwig Manuscripts
- Old Masters' drawings
- French decorative arts
- *Irises*, Van Gogh

TIPS

- Free art and exhibit tours depart Tue–Sat 11 and 1.30.
- Free architecture tours are six times a day.
- Free garden tours depart four times daily.
- Audioguides (inexpensive) are available in the entrance hall.

Carved into the foothills of West LA's Santa Monica Mountains, Richard Meier's Getty Center impresses visitors with its breathtaking architecture, city views and art.

Background Oil billionaire J. Paul Getty began collecting in the 1930s and a passion for Greek and Roman antiquities inspired the Getty Villa in Malibu (▷ 26–27). After his death in 1976 and his $700 million bequest, the size of its collections swelled. Opened in 1997, the $1 billion Getty Center houses Western art from the Middle Ages to the present, as well as the J. Paul Getty Trust's arts, education, research and funding projects.

Treasure Part fortress, part piazza, and focus of the 110-acre (45ha) complex, the inside-out

Clockwise from far left: Notable works of art collected by J. Paul Getty grace this architectural gem; visitors begin their tour in the museum entrance hall; the East building with views across the city and the Santa Monica foothills; Arii Matamoe (The Royal End), 1892, by Paul Gauguin

architecture is a triumph. Five honey-colored pavilions flank the central courtyard. The first four display the collections in chronological order; decorative arts and sculpture are on the first floor and paintings from the corresponding period on the upper level; the fifth pavilion houses special exhibitions.

Art First you will see medieval and Renaissance works, from illuminated manuscripts to the works of Fra Angelico. Next, stroll by the Old Masters, including Titian, Brueghel and Rembrandt. There are also English portraits, grand galleries of 18th-century French decorative arts, 19th- and 20th-century photographs—and Van Gogh's *Irises*. Step outside to the café or to explore the geometric plantings and soundscapes in the garden.

THE BASICS

www.getty.edu

🔁 D5

✉ 1200 Getty Center Drive, off I-405/San Diego Freeway

☎ 310/440-7300

🕐 Tue–Fri, Sun 10–5.30, Sat 10–9. Closed national hols

🍴 Restaurant (reservations essential) and cafés

🚌 761

♿ Excellent

💰 Museum free. Parking moderate

❓ Audioguides, talks, concerts, films, art classes, family activities

TOP 25

The Getty Villa in Malibu reopened in January 2006 after a major overhaul. This cultural landmark vividly evokes the classical world in its landscape and architecture.

Background Constructed in the early 1970s, the Getty Villa underwent a face-lift after the opening of the stunning Getty Center (▷ 24–25). The Malibu site closed for eight years (many years longer than initially expected), but reopened to great fanfare. No expense was spared for the new Villa, which now houses more than 44,000 antiquities of European origin. The building resembles an ancient Roman villa—appropriately enough, as it is dedicated to Greek, Roman and Etruscan antiquities.

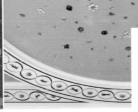

Clockwise from far left: Don't miss the stunning gardens, particularly the Outer Peristyle; Men in Antiquity Room, featuring the Wounded Youth Roman sculpture; Roman grave monument of a girl; ceiling detail at the entrance to the Getty Villa

Layout Visitors to the Villa walk through an open-air pavilion and then meander down a pathway to an impressive 450-seat outdoor classical theater. From the theater, visitors can enter the galleries or have lunch or a snack in the café. Twenty-three galleries display permanent works from the collection, while five other galleries showcase changing exhibitions. Antiquity, of course, is always the underlying theme.

Art More than 1,200 objects on display here range from the rare—*Victorious Youth*, aka the Getty Bronze, legal ownership of which is contested by Italy—to the ordinary, or rather, items that would have been ordinary to these ancient peoples, such as coins, vases and necklaces. The works date from 6,500BC to AD400.

THE BASICS

www.getty.edu

✚ A7

✉ 17985 Pacific Coast Highway, Pacific Palisades (access from northbound only)

☎ 310/440-7300

🕐 Wed–Mon 10–5. Closed national hols

🍽 Café; pre-order picnic lunches also available

🚌 534. You must have your advance admission ticket punched by the driver to enter the Villa

♿ Excellent

🎫 Museum free, but you need an advance, timed ticket (reserve ahead). Parking moderate

❓ Audioguides, talks, concerts

HIGHLIGHTS

● Playing drums, electric guitars and keyboards in the Roland Live exhibit
● Watching intimate live performances at the Clive Davis Theater

TIPS

● Check online calendars to plan your visit around major sporting events.
● Museum admission is discounted after 6pm on special public program nights.
● On-site parking garages cost $10–$25 ($5 for 2 hours or less).

Nowhere is LA's celebration of pop culture more alive than at this high-tech, modern museum. It's a shrine to all things rock "n" roll—pop, jazz, country, folk, blues, Latin and hip-hop, too.

Musical landscape Opened in 2008—just in time for the 50th anniversary of the GRAMMY Awards—this four-story museum takes visitors on an interactive journey through the history of American music, from early swing jazz and blues through late-20th-century urban sounds such as rap and grunge rock. In more than 30,000sq ft (2,787sq m) of exhibition space, touch-screen displays explore highlights by genre and geography: Listen to early Chicago and Memphis sounds, then fast-forward to today's Latin grooves.

Clockwise from left: A look behind the industries producers; the chic glass-fronted entrance to the museum; the Roland Live exhibition, giving people a chance to make their own music; costumes seen on the GRAMMY Awards red carpet; Culture Shock exhibit

American idols The priceless memorabilia here includes opera tenor Luciano Pavarotti's tux and Elvis's guitar. Explore seminal moments in pop music, like John Lennon's songwriting hits. Step into individual studio booths, where interactive videos of star singers, DJs and producers walk you through the recording process. Lay down a vocal track, then try remixing a dance club hit. Video screens replay the GRAMMY's greatest performances.

After dark The campus of L.A. Live, Downtown's newest entertainment complex, is anchored by the Staples Center (▷ 136) and Nokia Theatre. Bars, cafés, restaurants, a bowling alley, cinema and Latin-flavored nightclub co-owned by celebrities Jennifer Lopez and will.i.am are reasons to play here after dark.

THE BASICS

www.grammymuseum.org
www.lalive.com

✚ K6

✉ 800 W. Olympic Boulevard, Downtown

☎ 213/765-6800

🕐 Mon–Fri 11.30–7.30, Sat–Sun 10–7.30. Closed for some special events

🍴 Restaurants, cafés, bars

🚇 Pico

🚌 DASH F, 81, 460

♿ Very good

💲 Moderate

HIGHLIGHTS

- The tortilla-making machine near the entrance
- Great prices on produce and a huge variety of foods

TIPS

- Park at 308 S. Hill Street. The first hour is free if you spend $10. Validate the parking ticket at the information desk.
- Try the Mexican hot chocolate–or an item you've never heard of!

Sawdust coats the floor and butchers' knives chop-chop and thud away on a dozen counters, just as they have since 1917 at this bustling Downtown landmark.

Downtown's historic larder LA's largest and oldest food market, a maze of closely packed stalls, first opened its doors in 1917, and the hangar-like building has been feeding the Downtown district ever since. In those days, Broadway was LA's poshest thoroughfare, while today it is the heart of the city's crowded Latino shopping district. The market goes from busy to heaving on Saturday, when the noise and the bustle is unbelievable.

Chilies and cacti For anyone who loves food or markets, Grand Central is a real find. A

Clockwise from left: Grand Central Market in full swing; the Broadway entrance to the market; chefs preparing tortillas at a take-out stand

fantastic feast for the eyes, it is also a great place to grab picnic food or stop for a snack. Chili peppers, avocados and big beef tomatoes are stacked into glossy piles alongside stalks of celery, potatoes in myriad hues, huge bunches of bananas and pyramids of oranges, lemons and apples. Among the less familiar offerings are prickly pears, cactus leaves and dozens of different types of fresh and dried chilies in varying degrees of ferocity. There are around 50 stalls in all, including fish merchants and tortilla makers, confectioners, delicatessens selling cheese and cold meats, spice merchants, dried fruit and nut sellers and the Chinese herbalist. Take-out food stands do a roaring trade in Mexican snacks, and there are quick-bite stops with tables and chairs for customers to use near the Hill Street exit.

THE BASICS

www.grandcentralsquare.
com
✚ L6
✉ 317 S. Broadway
☎ 213/624-2378
🕐 Daily 9–6
🍴 Several Mexican
fast-food take-out stands,
Chinese noodle café, deli,
bakery and a juice bar
🚇 Civic Center, Pershing
Square
🚌 DASH D
♿ Few
🎟 Free

HIGHLIGHTS

● Planetarium show at the Observatory
● Views of LA from the Observatory's terraces and roof deck
● Outdoor activities in the park

TIP

● After a five-year, $93-million renovation, the Observatory draws big crowds. Reservations are not required, but parking is limited and an uphill walk to the Observatory may be required.

A vast open-air park straddling the Hollywood Hills, Griffith Park offers a raft of activities, the Museum of the American West and, from its landmark Observatory, the best view of the Hollywood sign.

A handsome bequest The largest municipal park in the United States, Griffith Park lies in the foothills of the Santa Monica Mountains. The original 3,015-acre (1,220ha) site was given to the city in 1896 by Col. Griffith Jenkins Griffith, who also left a trust with sufficient funds to build the amphitheater-style Greek Theater in 1930, a favorite outdoor concert venue, and the Griffith Observatory, which overlooks the city and houses an astronomy museum. The Observatory includes the Zeiss telescope, solar telescopes and

Clockwise from far left: A monument to notable scientists in Griffith Park; there are great views of LA from the park's walking trails; the Hollywood sign keeps watch over visitors to the park; the black dome of the observatory; a distant view of the observatory high on the hills above the city

laser projection shows at the Samuel Oschin Planetarium (▷ 135). Sharing public space in the park is the Autry National Center–Museum of the American West (▷ 66), cofounded by actor Gene Autry, and the Los Angeles Zoo (▷ 69).

Around the park The park offers a variety of scenery. You can walk the leafy Ferndell trail or reach the rugged high chaparral by a network of trails and easy-to-follow fire roads (maps from the Ranger Station). In the southeast corner of the park, near the Los Feliz exit, there are miniature train rides and children's pony rides. The antique merry-go-round, near the central Ranger Station, is adored by small children, and there are picnic areas, tennis courts and golf courses with plenty of parking nearby.

THE BASICS

www.laparks.org
www.griffithobservatory.org
✚ J3 K4
✉ Off I–5/Golden State Freeway and 134/Ventura Freeway in the north
☎ Ranger Station: 323/913-4688. Observatory: 213/473-0800
🕐 Daily 5am–10.30pm (trails and mountain roads close at sunset). Observatory: Wed–Fri 12–10, Sat–Sun 10–10. Merry-go-round: Sat–Sun 11–5, daily in summer
🍴 Refreshment stands
🚌 96, DASH Weekend Observatory Shuttle
♿ Observatory: excellent. Park: good to nonexistent
💲 Park and Observatory: free. Fees for other attractions, including planetarium

HIGHLIGHTS

- Mann's Chinese Theatre
- Hollywood Walk of Fame
- The historic Hollywood Roosevelt Hotel (▷ 157)

TIP

- If you want to visit a number of Hollywood attractions, consider the Hollywood CityPass ($59 for adults, $39 for children aged 3–11). Visit www. citypass.com/hollywood for more information.

Though Hollywood Boulevard's 1930s and 1940s heyday is a distant memory, the Hollywood and Highland center and the return of the Academy Awards have put some of the glitz back.

Face-lift After 50 years of decline, Tinseltown's most evocative address is undergoing a major face-lift. One of the first things to be buffed up has been the corner of Hollywood Boulevard and Highland Avenue. Next to Mann's Chinese Theatre, the Hollywood and Highland center (▷ 118), a five-floor, open-air retail and entertainment complex, bedazzles with its fine stores, restaurants and a grand staircase that leads to a panoramic view of the Hollywood sign. The 3,500-seat Kodak Theatre is now the home for the Academy Awards ceremony.

From far left: Crowds gather outside Mann's Chinese Theatre; looking down over Hollywood Walk of Fame; one of the city's best viewpoints, looking out at the Hollywood Sign from the Hollywood and Highland center

Everyone is invited to place their hands, feet, hooves or (in the case of Betty Grable) legs in those of the stars, in the concrete courtyard of Mann's Chinese Theatre. Booths sell self-guiding Hollywood star site maps, although they're not always accurate.

Hollywood history Sid Grauman, who built the Chinese Theatre, was also one of the founding partners in the Hollywood Roosevelt Hotel (▷ 157) across the street. A couple of Michelle Pfeiffer's nightclub scenes from *The Fabulous Baker Boys* (1989) were filmed here. The Capitol Records Tower (▷ 67) is a famous landmark. An assortment of celebrity figures can be found in the Hollywood Wax Museum at No. 6767, while star memorabilia awaits at the Hollywood Museum (▷ 68–69).

THE BASICS

➕ H5–J5

Visitor Information Center
www.discoverlosangeles.com
✉ Hollywood and Highland, 6801 Hollywood Boulevard
☎ 323/467-6412
🕐 Mon–Sat 10–10, Sun 10–7
🚇 Metro Red Line
🚌 DASH Hollywood, 217, 780
♿ Free

HIGHLIGHTS

● Ellesmere Chaucer and illuminated manuscripts
● *Pinkie*, Sir Thomas Lawrence
● Refurbished 1911 Beaux Arts mansion interiors
● *The Long Leg*, Hopper
● Japanese gardens
● Jungle garden, desert garden and lily ponds

TIP

● There is a free garden tour Mon, Wed–Fri 12–2, Sat–Sun 10.30–2.30 (depends on availability of volunteers).

Three elements—manuscripts, paintings and gardens—contribute to this rich and varied experience, and there hardly seems enough time to do each of them justice.

Collectors Henry E. Huntington (1850–1927) moved to LA in 1902 and made a second fortune organizing the city's rail system. When he retired, to devote himself to his library, he married his uncle's widow, Arabella, who shared his interest in art. Together they amassed 18th-century British portraits, French furnishings and decorative arts, bequeathing them for public benefit.

Manuscripts The Library building's extraordinary treasury of rare and precious manuscripts and books spans over 800 years, from the famous

Clockwise from top left: The Gutenburg Bible; cacti growing in the Desert Garden; the Japanese Garden, one of the highlights of a visit; the mansion housing the Huntington's European art collections; view across the lake to the Terrace of the Jade Mirror in the Chinese Garden

15th-century Ellesmere Chaucer and a Gutenberg Bible on vellun to a rare edition of naturalist John James *Audubon's Birds of America*.

Fine art The 1911 Beaux Arts mansion displays the famous portrait collection, including Gainsborough's *Blue Boy*. Here, too, you will find ornate French furnishings and porcelain, and 18th-century European paintings added since Huntington's day. American art features furnishings from the Arts and Crafts team Greene and Greene (▷ 6).

Glorious gardens Huntington began work on the spectacular gardens in collaboration with William Hertrich in 1904. Today, there are about 14,000 types of plants and trees in 15 separate areas, including a rose garden.

THE BASICS

www.huntington.org

➕ Q5

✉ 1151 Oxford Road, San Marino (Pasadena)

☎ 626/405-2100

🕐 Mon, Wed–Fri 12–4.30, Sat–Sun 10.30–4.30. Holiday Mons 10.30–4.30. Closed national hols except Easter

🍴 Tearoom and café

🚌 ARTS 10

♿ Good

💲 Expensive. Free first Thu of month

● Model of a trapped mammoth in Lake Pit

TIP

● Excavations are still ongoing at the Tar Pits. Most recently paleon-tologists have worked at Pit 91 behind the museum, where more exciting discoveries may be made.

It's hard to imagine in the conurbation of today, but during the last Ice Age the Los Angeles Basin teemed with wolves, saber-toothed tigers and mammoths. Proof of their presence is in their bones, more than a million of which have been interred precisely where they died, in the primal black ooze of La Brea Tar Pits.

The famous tar pits Oozing from a fissure in the earth's crust, these gooey black tar pits (*brea* is Spanish for tar) are one of the world's most famous fossil sites. For thousands of years during the last great Ice Age, plants, birds and animals have been trapped and entombed here, turning the asphalt into a paleontological soup from which scientists have recovered millions of

Clockwise from far left: A mammoth model displayed at the Tar Pits; natural gas bubble slowly escaping from the Tar Pits; a reconstruction of a Columbia mammoth skeleton; the view across La Brea Tar Pits toward Los Angeles Country Museum of Art on Wilshire Boulevard

fossilized remnants from some 231 species of vertebrates and 159 types of plant. Most of the fossils date from 10,000 to 40,000 years ago. The pits are fenced in and are attractive neither to look at nor to smell, but they are surrounded by pleasant Hancock Park, where you can stroll and take a picnic.

Page Museum The museum opened in 1977 to provide explanation and context to the bones and fossils pulled out of the pits. Here you can see reconstructed skeletons of extinct species like saber-toothed tigers and giant sloths. There is also a short film about the history of the digs—excavation dates back to 1906—and a Paleontology Laboratory, where visitors can watch scientists in action classifying and cleaning the uncovered bones.

THE BASICS

www.tarpits.org

+ H6

✉ The George C. Page Museum at the La Brea Tar Pits, 5801 Wilshire Boulevard, Mid-City

☎ 323/934-7243

◉ Daily 9.30–5. Guided tours of tar pits Tue–Sun at 1, of museum Tue–Sun at 2 (volunteer guides permitting). Closed national hols

🚌 DASH Fairfax, 20, 217, 720, 780

♿ Good

💰 Moderate. Free 1st Tue of month

14 LA County Arboretum & Botanic Garden

- Queen Anne Cottage
- Santa Anita Railroad Depot
- Bird-watching
- Blooming pink trumpet trees in March, irises in April and jacaranda trees in June
- Mayberg Waterfall

Set against the backdrop of the San Gabriel Mountains, these lovely gardens, in a corner of the old Rancho Santa Anita, offer year-round color and interest.

Mexican rancho Rancho Santa Anita was one of several ranches in the valley when Hugo Reid built his adobe house here in 1840. Furnished in simple pioneer style, it is one of three historic buildings in the grounds. The others are silver-mining millionaire E. J. "Lucky" Baldwin's fairy-tale 1885 Victorian cottage and the 1890 Santa Anita Railroad Depot.

From *Acacia* to *Ziziphus* The lush profusion of trees and plants (the arboretum is a favorite exotic movie location) includes jungle areas, towering palms, splashing waterfalls and

Clockwise from left: The Mayberg Waterfall; the San Gabriel Mountains provide an idyllic setting; peacocks are one of the delights found at the Arboretum; the Queen Anne guest house in the grounds of the Arboretum

quiet corners to enjoy the peace—as long as the raucous peacocks (introduced by Lucky Baldwin) are silent. Seek out the aquatic garden, the tropical greenhouse, the demonstration home gardens and the California landscape area, which shows the valley's natural state. There is much to see, so consider taking a tram tour to the farther reaches of the grounds (127 acres/51.4ha). The Arboretum also offers a variety of special events, from one-day classes to lectures to family treasure hunts. Check the website for dates and information.

More gardens in the area About 12 miles (19km) away is Descanso Gardens (1418 Descanso Drive, La Cañada Flintridge; tel 818/949-4200; www.descansogardens.org), 150 acres (61ha) of lovely landscaped property.

THE BASICS

www.arboretum.org

➕ S3

🏢 301 N. Baldwin Road, Arcadia (off I-210)

☎ 626/821-3222

🕐 Daily 9–5 (last ticket sales 4.30). Closed Christmas

🍴 Peacock café

🚌 FT187

♿ Few

💲 Moderate; free 3rd Tue of month (no tram)

❓ Regular tram tours visit the extensive grounds

HIGHLIGHTS

● Annual cherry blossom festival in early April
● A performance by the East West Players
● The Go for Broke Monument, which commemorates nearly 16,000 Japanese American World War II veterans
● The annual festival Nisei Week in August, with floats, a parade, cultural exhibits, Japanese food and more

TIP

● Check www.jaccc.org for information about upcoming events and performances.

The hub of LA's Japanese American community is fairly low-key and walkable. You'll find surprise outposts of Japanese landscaping tucked into the concrete jungle.

Historical notes Bounded by 1st and 3rd, Los Angeles and Alameda streets, this area was first settled at the end of the 19th century. Several historic buildings remain on 1st Street, which leads to the Japanese American National Museum (▷ 69).

Sushi and shiatsu Over the road, among the neat pompoms of pollarded trees and bright blue tile roofs, Japanese Village Plaza's 40 restaurants and small shops, exotic supermarkets and sushi bars make for interesting browsing and snacking. You can then cross

Japanese Village Plaza

Clockwise from far left: Detail of a panel displaying Japanese characters within the Higashi Honganji Buddhist Temple; a Yagura, fire lookout tower, on Japanese Village Plaza; paper lanterns are strung out across the streets of Little Tokyo; James Irvine Garden

2nd Street for the Japanese American Cultural and Community Center, where the Doizaki Gallery exhibits Japanese artworks. The adjacent Aratani/Japan America Theatre (▷ 129) presents contemporary and traditional Japanese performances such as Noh and Kabuki theater productions. Outside, a 1,000ft (304m) installation commemorates a timeline spanning six decades of Japanese American history.

Garden oasis Another feature of the plaza is the delightful James Irvine Garden, a Japanese-style oasis encircled by a stream, with paths, bridges, stepping stones, trees and flowering shrubs such as azaleas. There is more elegant Japanese landscaping nearby, outside the graceful Higashi Honganji Buddhist Temple at No. 505 E. 3rd Street.

THE BASICS

www.visitlittletokyo.com
🔲 L6
🚌 DASH A

Japanese American Cultural and Community Center
www.jaccc.org
✉ Noguchi Plaza, 244 S. San Pedro Street
☎ 213/628-2725
🕐 Doizaki Gallery: Tue–Fri 12–5, Sat–Sun 11–4

An easy day trip south from central Los Angeles, Long Beach has plenty to offer—from the regal *Queen Mary* and jam-packed aquarium to water sports, shopping and gondola rides.

On the water A convenient first stop at the foot of the freeway, the *Queen Mary* finally came to rest here in 1967. What was once the largest liner afloat is now a hotel, and audio and guided tours give access to the engine rooms, cabin suites and gorgeous art-deco salons. Across the Queensway Bay Bridge (AquaBus water taxi available), the excellent Aquarium of the Pacific showcases nearly 500 marine species from the northern Pacific to the tropics, including sharks, giant octopuses and California sea lions. East from here, Shoreline Drive skirts

Clockwise from far left: Queen Mary *takes pride of place at Long Beach; the* Aquarium of the Pacific *is a big draw; Tichenor House; the brightly painted Meladrama Theater is a sunny sight at Shoreline Village; boats moored in the harbor at Shoreline Village*

THE BASICS

✚ Off map, south

Long Beach Area Convention & Visitors Bureau
www.visitlongbeach.com
✉ 301 E. Ocean Boulevard
☎ 562/436-3645, 800/452-7829
🕐 Mon–Fri 8–5
🚇 Metro Blue Line

The *Queen Mary*
www.queenmary.com
✉ 1126 Queens Highway, Long Beach
☎ 562/435-3511
🕐 Daily 10–6 (extended hours for restaurants, bars, lounges and evening tours)
🚍 Passport C
♿ Few
💲 Expensive

Aquarium of the Pacific
www.aquariumofpacific.org
✉ 100 Aquarium Way, Long Beach
☎ 562/590-3100
🕐 Daily 9–6
🚍 Passport C
♿ Very good
💲 Expensive

San Pedro Bay, passing the Long Beach Arena, encircled by the world's biggest mural, *Planet Ocean*, by the marine artist Wyland. Shoreline Village is popular for shopping, dining, boat trips and views of the *Queen Mary*.

Downtown to Venice Island Pine Avenue, at the heart of Downtown Long Beach, bustles with shops and restaurants. Take Ocean Drive east to Belmont Shores, where concessionaires rent out water-sports equipment, and bicycles and skates for riding the beach path. Behind the beach, 2nd Street has shops and restaurants, and crosses on to Naples Island. This affluent residential neighborhood, crisscrossed with canals, was developed in the 1920s. Explore it on foot, or indulge in a relaxing ride with Gondola Getaway, tel 562/433-9595.

HIGHLIGHTS

● Drawings by Degas
● Edo scrolls and netsuke, Japanese Pavilion
● Paintings and drawings by Kandinsky and Rodchenko
● *The Treachery of Images (This is Not a Pipe)*, Magritte
● Persian illuminated manuscripts
● *Untitled*, Rothko
● *Nympheas*, Monet

TIPS

● Free gallery tours and talks are given several times daily.
● Check the website for live music, films and lectures.

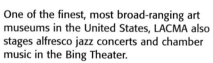

One of the finest, most broad-ranging art museums in the United States, LACMA also stages alfresco jazz concerts and chamber music in the Bing Theater.

The collections The majority of the museum's permanent collections are housed in the Ahmanson Building. Here magnificent examples of ancient Asian, Egyptian and pre-Columbian art, medieval and Renaissance paintings, works by 17th-century Dutch landscape specialists and 18th-century French Romantics have been gathered together with a feast of Impressionist, Fauvist, Cubist and Surrealist art. There is a dazzling array of European and American decorative arts, plus costumes and textiles, jewel-like Persian manuscripts and Ottoman ceramics.

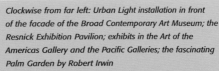

Clockwise from far left: Urban Light installation in front of the facade of the Broad Contemporary Art Museum; the Resnick Exhibition Pavilion; exhibits in the Art of the Americas Gallery and the Pacific Galleries; the fascinating Palm Garden by Robert Irwin

Exhibitions and sculpture gardens In addition to housing selections from the permanent collections, the Art of the Americas and Hammer buildings offer special display space. So does the bold Broad Contemporary Art Museum, which draws from LACMA's international collections of paintings, sculptures, film and video, conceptual works and installation art. Catch special exhibitions in the new Resnick Exhibition Pavilion nearby. The entire campus is enhanced by outdoor sculpture gardens.

Make a plan The museum complex is spread over seven buildings. Its collections are so vast that there is too much to be seen comfortably in a single visit, so it is advisable to plot a route around personal favorites with the aid of a lay-out plan from the ticket booth at the entrance.

THE BASICS

www.lacma.org

➕ 116

🖼 5905 Wilshire Boulevard, Mid-City

☎ 323/857-6000

🕐 Mon–Tue, Thu 12–8, Fri 12–9, Sat–Sun 11–8. Closed Thanksgiving, Christmas

🍴 Restaurants and café

🚌 DASH Fairfax, 20, 217, 720, 780

♿ Very good

💲 Moderate. Free 2nd Tue of month and some Mon national hols

18 Melrose Avenue and Mid-City Shopping Spree

HIGHLIGHTS

● Under-the-radar boutiques and vintage clothing finds on Melrose Avenue
● Star-spotting on Robertson Boulevard and Rodeo Drive

TIPS

● Some boutiques close on Sunday and Monday.
● LA's Original Farmers' Market (▷ 116) on W. 3rd Street is a touristy, but fun, place to take a quick break and eat outdoors.

Melrose Avenue is a 3-mile (5km) strip of esoteric and exotic buys, from cutting-edge fashion and retro wear to art and whimsical gifts. Other shopping streets around Mid-City also enchant fashionistas.

High/low fashion finds Whether you're looking for a bargain on a 1950s pin-up dress or a pair of $600 stiletto heels, tempting buys and glitzy baubles await on Melrose Avenue. East of Fairfax Avenue, vintage clothing stores like Wasteland (▷ 123) rub shoulders with "pop-up" shops by emerging designers from SoCal and abroad, especially Japan. West of Fairfax, Melrose Avenue turns more upscale, with high-end boutiques, specialty shops and art and design galleries clustered around La Cienega Boulevard.

Clockwise from far left: Mannequins in the window of Wasteland on Melrose Avenue; happy shoppers after a visit to Urban Outfitters; the Spanish Steps off Rodeo Drive; Kitson boutique, another trendy store on Melrose Avenue

Boulevard boutiques Art galleries and one-of-a-kind boutiques stocking retro and prêt-à-porter wear line laid-back La Brea Avenue, south of Melrose. Elsewhere, celebrities go power shopping along a short, star-studded stretch of Robertson Boulevard behind the giant Beverly Center mall (▷ 115). LA designers Kitson (▷ 118) and Lisa Kline (▷ 119) are landmarks on the boulevard, along with European designers like Chanel and Armani.

Beverly Hills For black-belt window-shopping, Beverly Hills lies farther west. Beverly Hills' "Golden Triangle" is a showpiece of brand-name designer emporiums. Prada Epicenter (343 N. Rodeo Drive) was designed by postmodern architect Rem Koolhaas. Exclusive department stores line well-heeled Wilshire Boulevard.

THE BASICS

www.discoverlosangeles.com/play/shopping

🔲 F5–I6

🚌 DASH Fairfax, 10, 16, 220

HIGHLIGHTS

Works by:
● de Kooning
● Giacometti
● Mondrian
● Pollock
● Oldenburg

TIPS

● The entry ticket gains you admission to both main museums.
● Parking (moderate) is available at the Walt Disney Concert Hall garage with museum validation.

A single museum with two addresses a mile (1.6km) apart, and a third across town, MOCA has a growing catalog of post-1940 artworks that constitutes one of the most important contemporary art collections in the US.

Downtown From the outside, MOCA at California Plaza, designed by Japanese architect Arata Isozaki, is a constructing of geometric cubes and pyramids clad in red brick, while the inside is all blond wood and vast white spaces—a fitting environment for the pieces on display. MOCA's downtown gallery presents a changing schedule of both shows drawn from the extensive permanent collection and touring exhibitions. The busy calendar also introduces newly commissioned

From far left: An outdoor art installation by Nancy Rubins, made of used plane parts; the impressive museum building is a fitting home for the pieces on display; Water Cascade, a stunning display outside the museum

works by established and emerging artists in a broad variety of media. The emphasis may be on temporary exhibitions, but there is also a strong permanent collection, with works by de Kooning, Lichtenstein, Arbus, Rothko and Warhol, among others.

Around town While Isozaki's museum was under construction, MOCA transformed a spacious warehouse in Little Tokyo into gallery space, now known as the Geffen Contemporary at MOCA. The vast industrial space, with its ramps and girders, is ideal for displaying big installation pieces. Smaller works occupy a maze of galleries overlooked from a mezzanine level. Across town is a third gallery (free) at the Pacific Design Center (8687 Melrose Avenue, West Hollywood).

THE BASICS

MOCA

www.moca.org

🔠 L6

✉ 250 S. Grand Avenue

☎ 213/626-6222

🕐 Mon, Fri 11–5, Thu 11–8, Sat–Sun 11–6. Closed national hols

🚇 Metro Red Line

🚌 DASH B

♿ Very good

💲 Moderate (free Thu 5–8)

Geffen Contemporary

🔠 L6

✉ 152 N. Central Avenue

🕐 Same as MOCA

🚌 DASH A

20 Natural History Museum of LA County

- Insect Zoo
- Megamouth, the rarest shark in the world
- Shreiber Hall of Birds

- A free gallery tour is available daily at 2pm.
- If you're driving, bring cash for parking (credit cards are not accepted).

Enjoy a collection that dates back 4.5 billion years at this imaginatively designed museum, which also houses engaging exhibits from California's and LA's more recent past.

The broad picture The Natural History Museum of LA County is a handsome Spanish Renaissance Revival affair on the north side of Exposition Park. Its wide-ranging collections cover not only natural history but also superb Mesoamerican artifacts, including gold jewelry and pottery from the Maya, Inca and Aztec cultures; an excellent Native American section with Zuni fetishes; and intricate Plains Indian beadwork and Navajo textiles. There are also galleries dedicated to California and American history.

Left: *Tyrannosaurus rex and Triceratops skeletons;*
below: *Colorful stained-glass in the museum's central dome*

The natural wonders Always popular, the newly reopened Dinosaur Hall displays over 300 fossils, including 20 full-body skeletons and the world's only growth series of tyrannosaurus rex, which features a baby, juvenile and adult. Equally impressive is the reconstruction of triceratops, a three-horned herbivore with a large bony frill. The wildlife dioramas in the North American and African Mammal halls display animals from polar bears to zebras. On the geological front, there is a Gem and Mineral Hall, and in the Discovery Center there are touchy-feely games and toys, fossil rubbings and other hands-on diversions. The mezzanine level houses the Insect Zoo with a creepy-crawly collection including hissing cockroaches from Madagascar, pink-toed tarantulas and nauseating assassin bugs.

THE BASICS

www.nhm.org

☩ K8

✉ 900 Exposition Boulevard

☎ 213/763-3466

🕐 Daily 9.30–5. Closed July 4, Thanksgiving, Christmas, Jan 1

🍴 Cafeteria

🚇 Metro Expo Line

🚌 DASH F/Expo Park, 38

♿ Very good

✋ Moderate

HIGHLIGHTS

- *Branchini Madonna*, Giovanni di Paolo
- *Portrait of a Boy*, Rembrandt
- *Burghers of Calais*, Rodin
- *The Stone Breakers, Le Raincy*, Seurat
- *Exotic Landscape*, Rousseau
- *Flower Vendor (Girl with Lilies)*, Rivera
- Japanese woodblock prints
- *Woman with a Book*, Picasso
- Degas Collection

Though the collections gathered here are not as well known as those in the Getty Center and LACMA, many prized world-famous artworks found here make this small museum one of LA's best.

History The collections were originally founded as the Pasadena Art Institute in 1924. Under the direction of wealthy industrialist and collector Norton Simon (1907–93), the museum grew into a world-class collection of European Old Masters, Impressionist and Postimpressionist works, as well as Asian sculpture, arranged around a sculpture garden.

History of art The collections begin with jewel-like 14th-century Italian religious paintings and Renaissance art. The ravishing *Branchini*

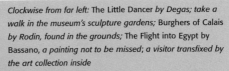
Clockwise from far left: The Little Dancer by Degas; take a walk in the museum's sculpture gardens; Burghers of Calais by Rodin, found in the grounds; The Flight into Egypt by Bassano, a painting not to be missed; a visitor transfixed by the art collection inside

Madonna is just one of the highlights; the collection includes works by Filippino Lippi, Botticelli, Bellini and Cranach the Elder. From the 17th and 18th centuries there are Rembrandt portraits; Canaletto's minutely detailed Venetian scenes; soft, plump Tiepolo figures; and Rubens' oils on a heroic scale. The superb 19th- to 20th-century galleries show major works by Monet, Renoir, Cézanne and van Gogh, and a fistful of color from Matisse, Kandinsky, Braque and Klee. The superb Degas Collection includes rare landscapes, enigmatic monotypes and an exceptional series of bronze dancers posthumously cast from wax models found in the artist's studio. The museum also possesses a rich collection of excellent Hindu and Buddhist sculpture from Nepal, India, Thailand and Cambodia.

THE BASICS

www.nortonsimon.org
✚ P3
✉ 411 W. Colorado Boulevard, Pasadena
☎ 626/449-6840
🕐 Wed–Mon 12–6 (Fri until 9)
🚇 Metro Gold Line
🚌 180, 181; ARTS 10
♿ Good
✋ Moderate

HIGHLIGHTS

● Pacific Coast Bicycle Path
● Santa Monica Pier
● The sunset from Palisades Park, on Ocean Avenue, between Colorado Avenue and San Vincente Boulevard
● Third Street Promenade

Tanned bodies playing volleyball and the crowded bicycle path, plus great shopping and drinking on the bustling promenade, draw crowds to this enduringly popular stretch of coast.

Pier pressure Santa Monica's landmark 1909 pier still exudes an old-fashioned amusement-park aura that evokes a fuzzy nostalgia in adults and requests for money from attendant offspring. Along the weathered wooden board-walk, Pacific Park's (▷ 134) giant Ferris wheel and roller coaster loom above the restored 1922 carousel operated by Paul Newman in the movie, *The Sting*. Down at beach level, the Santa Monica Pier Aquarium presents marine exhibits, aquariums and touch tanks. You can also rent a bicycle or in-line skates to swoop

Clockwise from top left: Gymnasts perform at the original Muscle Beach, Santa Monica; visitors stroll up and down Third Street Promenade, Santa Monica; riding the waves at Malibu; looking down over Malibu Colony, home to the stars; the Ferris wheel, a Santa Momica Pier landmark

along the 8.5-mile (14km) paved coastal path all the way to Venice Beach (▷ 62–63).

Beyond the beach Santa Monica's inland entertainment hub is Third Street Promenade, four pedestrian-only blocks of stores, cafés and movie theaters. For a more esoteric experience, visit Main Street (between Hollister and Rose avenues), with its restaurants, boutiques and galleries, and the California Heritage Museum.

Along the coast Quieter and more remote than Santa Monica, its neighbor, the enclave of Malibu, lures visitors with its 27 miles (43km) of sprawling beaches and canyons. Despite its drawbacks—traffic, brush fires and mud slides— plenty of Hollywood luminaries hang their hats here. The real draw is the surfing.

THE BASICS

Santa Monica
www.santamonica.com
🚇 D7

Malibu
www.malibu.org
🚇 Off map, west of A7

🛈 Santa Monica Visitor Center, 1920 Main Street, tel 310/393-7593 or 800/544-5319, daily 9–5.30; also kiosks at 1400 Ocean Avenue (at Santa Monica Boulevard in Palisades Park) and at 322 Santa Monica Pier
🍴 Restaurants, bars, cafés
🚌 704, 720; SM1, 2, 3, 7, 8, 9, 10
♿ Good to nonexistent, depending on location

- *Juno*, Rembrandt
- *Salome Dancing before Herod*, Moreau
- Grunwald Center exhibitions
- *Hospital at Saint-Rémy* and *The Sowers*, van Gogh
- *Boy Resting*, Cézanne

TIP

- Check the museum website for a calendar of lectures, films and live performances.

With a reputation for exhibitions that focus on lesser-known artists, the Hammer Museum is a dynamic cultural center in Westwood Village.

Hammer and tongs Oil billionaire Armand Hammer originally promised his art collections to a number of local institutions. To their chagrin, he then decided to found his own museum instead. The Hammer Museum opened in 1990, just three weeks before Hammer's death, with UCLA taking over the operation of the institution in 1994.

Minor miracles Modest in size, the Hammer is a respite from more overwhelming local museums. The Armand Hammer Collection is composed mainly of Impressionist and

Clockwise from far left: The Hammer Museum's facade; catch a film at the Billy Wilder Theater; exhibits are displayed in bright contemporary galleries or, in contrast, against rich dark backgrounds; the museum stages a program of lectures

Postimpressionist works by painters such as Degas, Pissarro, and van Gogh. In the Hammer Contemporary Collection the emphasis is on late 20th century and 21st century art. Artists represented include Ed Ruscha, Kara Walker and John Baldessari.

Graphic arts The museum is also a showcase for the Grunwald Center for the Graphic Arts. This collection consists of more than 45,000 prints, drawings, photographs and book illustrations, including works by Dürer, Cézanne, Hokusai and Hiroshige, and is displayed in other themed exhibitions.

The Billy Wilder Theater The state-of-the-art theater is one of the few theaters in the US able to screen films in their original formats.

THE BASICS

www.hammer.ucla.edu
➕ E6
🚇 10099 Wilshire Boulevard, Westwood
☎ 310/443-7000
🕐 Tue–Sat 11–7 (Thu until 9), Sun 11–5. Closed national hols
🍽 Courtyard café
🚌 20, 720; SM1, 2, 3
♿ Very good
💲 Moderate (free Thu)

HIGHLIGHTS

● Special Effects Stage
● The Simpsons–The Ride
● The Adventures of Curious George
● Jurassic Park–The Ride
● Revenge of the Mummy–The Ride
● Shrek 4-D
● The Studio Tour
● Terminator 2: 3D
● Universal's House of Horrors
● WaterWorld show

TIPS

● Online discounts are often available from the website.
● To avoid long lines, get a Front of Line Pass, which costs $119 and gets you priority boarding on all rides and reserved seating at all shows

The world's biggest motion picture studio and theme park is a great day out. The renowned Studio Tour, Jurassic Park–The Ride and The Simpsons–The Ride alone are worth the price of admission.

Back to the beginning Universal Studios' founder Carl Laemmle moved his movie studio facility just north of Hollywood in 1915 and inaugurated Universal Studios tours during the silent movie era. The arrival of the talkies put an end to live audiences here until 1964, when trolley tours began; trams are still used to circle the 415-acre (168ha) backlot.

Orientation The Studio Tour, narrated by actress and comedienne Whoopi Goldberg, includes original movie sets from Steven

Clockwise from top left: Exhibition of movie memorabilia; the central atrium inside CityWalk; the retro Universal Studios sign from the 1980s; the Globe fountain, a symbol of Universal Studios; model shark used in the film Jaws

Spielberg's *War of the Worlds*; a chase sequence inspired by *The Fast and the Furious: Tokyo Drift*; a simulated flash flood introduced by weatherman Al Roker; and classic locations from the *Psycho* house to the Grinch's Whoville. Tram tours depart from the Upper Lot, which is also home to The Simpsons–The Ride, Shrek 4-D and half a dozen great shows. Get insights into behind-the-scenes technology at the Special Effects Stage.

Take a ride A long escalator links the Upper Lot to the Lower Lot. Here, Universal's Jurassic Park—The Ride visits a land of five-story dinosaurs built with the help of aerospace scientists. Nearby is the Revenge of the Mummy–The Ride roller coaster and a new Transformers special-effects ride, which opened in 2011.

THE BASICS

www.universalstudios
hollywood.com

➕ H3

✉ 1000 Universal Center
Drive, Universal City

☎ 818/622-3801,
800/864-8377

🕐 Daily. Hours vary;
longer hours Jun–Aug and
Sat–Sun all year

🍴 Wide range of dining
and fast-food options

🚇 Metro Red Line:
Universal City, then free
shuttle bus

♿ Good

💰 Expensive; children
under 3 free

HIGHLIGHTS

● Muscle Beach
● Ocean Front Walk
● Venice Canal Walkway
(access from S. Venice
Boulevard)
● Venice boardwalk
● Venice Pier

TIP

● The sky is often overcast
in the mornings, especially
in spring and early
summer, so save your trip
to the beach until the
afternoon.

Best known for its beachfront boardwalk,
bohemian Venice Beach has a flourishing
artists' community, lovely outdoor dining
and recreational facilities. People-watching
is the number-one pastime.

The action Where Main crosses Rose Avenue,
Jonathan Borofsky's 30ft (9m) *Ballerina Clown*
figure greets visitors to Venice. It is an appropriate icon for this entertaining beach community,
a throwback to the psychedelic 1960s, com-
bined with the narcissism of Muscle Beach.
Ocean Front Walk is where it all hangs out, a
nonstop parade of scantily clad humanity, shiny
bodybuilders, funky street performers, tourists
and bustling market stalls. Consider renting a
bicycle or a pair of rollerblades and join the
masses traveling the boardwalk on two wheels.

Clockwise from far left: Get your skates on down at the beach; cooling down in the clear blue sea; a lifeguard station silouetted against a beautiful sunset; a surfer riding the waves off Venice Beach; LAPD police officers patrol Venice on horseback

Italian dream Developer Abbot Kinney created this American snapshot of Venice, Italy, in the early 1900s as a tribute to its European counterpart, and the Venice Canal Walkway, just inland from Ocean Front Walk, explores the quiet, canal-lined residential neighborhood that gave the area its name. Venice, California, has earned itself both starring roles and bit parts in various films—as the seedy backdrop in Orson Welles' *Touch of Evil*, for example, and as the home of the fictitious Rydell High in the 1970s musical film *Grease*, starring John Travolta and Olivia Newton-John.

Join the buzz Afterward, take a stroll down Main Street, the artery that connects Santa Monica and Venice, and check out the shops and galleries. Do exercise caution at night.

THE BASICS

www.venicechamber.net

+ D9

☎ Venice Chamber of Commerce: 310/822-5425

🚌 SM1, 2

♿ Good to nonexistent depending on location

More to See

This section contains other great places to visit if you have more time. Some are in the heart of the city while others are a short journey away, found under Further Afield. This chapter also has fantastic excursions that you should set aside a whole day to visit.

In the Heart of the City

AUTRY NATIONAL CENTER–MUSEUM OF THE AMERICAN WEST

www.theautry.org

Cofounded by Hollywood movie star Gene Autry, this museum presents a gold mine of Western art and artifacts dating from Native American and pioneer days through contemporary times. Tales of community and conquest are interwoven. Special events include live music, theater, films and videos, craft workshops and more family fun, especially on weekends.

🔲 K3 ⊠ 4700 Western Heritage Way, Griffith Park ☎ 323/667-2000 ⏰ Tue–Fri 10–4, Sat–Sun 11–5. Closed national hols 🍴 Café 🚌 96 💷 Moderate

BRADBURY BUILDING

In 1892 elderly mining millionaire Lewis Bradbury commissioned George Wyman to create a monument to his achievements. The resulting building stands out mainly for its soaring, light-filled atrium, as seen in many Hollywood movies such as *Chinatown* and *Blade Runner*.

🔲 L6 ⊠ 304 S. Broadway (access to lobby only) ☎ 213/626-1893 ⏰ Daily 9–5 🚇 Civic Center 🚌 DASH D 💷 Free

BROADWAY HISTORIC THEATRE DISTRICT

www.laconservancy.org

For movie fans with an interest in the early days, downtown Broadway is the place to find the movie palaces of yesteryear. Several, such as the Los Angeles (No. 615), the Palace (No. 630) and the Orpheum (No. 842), are still open for live shows. Reservations are required for guided Saturday walking tours.

🔲 L7 ⊠ Broadway, between 3rd and 9th streets ☎ LA Conservancy tour: 213/430-4219 🚇 Pershing Square 🚌 DASH D 💷 Free, tour moderate

CALIFORNIA SCIENCE CENTER

www.californiasciencecenter.org

Hands-on science, technology and environmental displays appeal to children here, plus an IMAX theater. Explore Earth's ecosystems, ride a high-wire bicycle and tour 50ft (15m) tall

Original stagecoach displayed in the Museum of the American West

Tess, a human-body simulator.
➕ K8 ✉ 39th and Figueroa streets
☎ 323/724-3623 🕐 Daily 10–5 🚇 Expo
Park/USC 🚌 DASH F/Expo Park 🎟 Free
(except IMAX theater)

CAPITOL RECORDS TOWER

www.hollywoodandvine.com
Welton Becket's 1954 tower
houses the company that can
list Sinatra and the Beach Boys
among its signings, and is one
of Hollywood's most famous
landmarks. Though the architect
denied it was intentional, it
resembles a stack of records
topped by a needle.
➕ J5 ✉ 1750 Vine Street, Hollywood
🚇 Metro Red Line 🚌 DASH Hollywood,
4, 210, 704

CATHEDRAL OF OUR LADY OF THE ANGELS

www.olacathedral.org
Spanish architect José Rafael
Moneo designed this cathedral,
which was completed in 2002 to
the tune of nearly $190 million
(it was built to replace another
cathedral that had been severely

damaged in the 1994 earthquake).
The angular, terra-cotta-colored
building contains a vast Dobson
pipe organ; note the tapestries
along the nave and behind the altar.
➕ L6 ✉ 555 W. Temple Street
☎ 213/680-5200 🕐 Mon–Fri 6.30–6,
Sat 9–6, Sun 7–6 🚌 DASH B 🎟 Free

CITY HALL

www.lacity.org
This monolith, the tallest building
in the city from 1928 to 1964
and "destroyed" in *War of the
Worlds*, is as familiar as the Daily
Planet building in the Superman
TV series, and has starred in many
other TV shows and films.
➕ L6 ✉ 200 N. Spring Street
☎ 213/485-2121 🚇 Civic Center
🚌 DASH A, B, D

EGYPTIAN THEATRE

www.americancinematheque.com
This 1922 movie palace, home to
Hollywood's first premiere (*Robin
Hood* starring Douglas Fairbanks),
has been restored to its original
grandeur. Visitors can view *Forever
Hollywood*, a 55-minute film about

Resembling a stack of records,
the Capitol Records Tower

City Hall on North Spring Street

Hollywood's celebrated history, narrated by Sharon Stone.

🚺 H5 ✉ 6712 Hollywood Boulevard, Hollywood ☎ 323/466-3456 ⚫ Call for showtimes 💵 Moderate 🚇 Hollywood/ Highland 🚌 DASH Hollywood, 217

FRANKLIN D. MURPHY SCULPTURE GARDEN

Sculptures by such artists as Noguchi, Arp and Hepworth are sprinkled liberally over the lawns. Works by Jacques Lipchitz, Henry Moore, Rodin, Alexander Calder and Maillol can be found on the tree-lined promenade.

🚺 E6 ✉ UCLA Campus off Charles E. Young Drive N. ☎ Tours: 310/443-755 ⚫ Open site 🚌 2, 302; SM1, 2, 3, 8, 12 (off Sunset Boulevard)

HOLLYWOOD FOREVER

www.hollywoodforever.com

Near Paramount Studios, this historical cemetery is the final resting place of Cecil B. DeMille, Jayne Mansfield, Rudolph Valentino and many other famous Hollywood actors. Pick up a gravesite map from the gift shop.

In summer, DJs spin and movies are screened outdoors.

🚺 J5 ✉ 6000 Santa Monica Boulevard, Hollywood ☎ 323/469-1181 ⚫ Daily 7–6 🚌 4 💵 Free

HOLLYWOOD HERITAGE MUSEUM

www.hollywoodheritage.org

Cecil B. De Mille shot Hollywood's first full-length movie in this old horse barn in 1913. Moved from its site on Vine Street to the Paramount, a lot across from the Hollywood Bowl (▷ 132), it now houses film memorabilia and antique movie-making equipment.

🚺 H4 ✉ 2100 N. Highland Avenue ☎ 323/874-2276 ⚫ Wed–Sun 12–4 🚌 156, 426 ♿ Few 💵 Moderate ❓ Heritage walking tour Sat 9am (☎ 323/465-6716 for reservations)

HOLLYWOOD MUSEUM

www.thehollywoodmuseum.com

Inside the 1935 art-deco Max Factor Building, walk through Hannibal Lecter's jail cell, then gawk at Marilyn Monroe's million-dollar dress, Rocky's

An exhibit in the Franklin D. Murphy Sculpture Garden

boxing gloves and Nicole Kidman's *Moulin Rouge* costumes. Hundreds of vintage and contemporary movie scripts, posters and celebrity photographs are on display.

✚ H5 ✉ 1660 N. Highland Avenue, Hollywood ☎ 323/464-7776 🕐 Wed–Sun 10–5 🚇 Hollywood/Highland 🚌 DASH Hollywood, 217, 780 💰 Expensive

JAPANESE AMERICAN NATIONAL MUSEUM

www.janm.org

Learn the story of Japanese migration to the US, and the Japanese Americans' struggle for acceptance in their adopted home. Moving exhibits deal with World War II internment camps.

✚ L6 ✉ 369 E. 1st Street ☎ 213/625-0414 🕐 Tue–Sun 11–5 (Thu until 8) 🚌 DASH A 💰 Moderate

KODAK THEATRE

www.kodaktheatre.com

Lacking an invite to the next Academy Awards? Content yourself with a behind-the-scenes guided tour of Hollywood's most glam theater, where Céline Dion, Alicia Keys and American Idol finalists have strutted on stage. Take a peek at VIP rooms and get close to a real Oscar statuette.

✚ H5 ✉ 6801 Hollywood Boulevard, Hollywood ☎ 323/308-6300 🕐 30-min tours daily 10.30–4 (closed for special events) 🚇 Hollywood/Highland 🚌 DASH Hollywood, 217, 780 💰 Expensive

LOS ANGELES ZOO

LA Zoo is filled with more than 1,100 animals from 250 species ranging from koalas to Komodo dragons, so there's plenty to see. In the mid-1990s the zoo faced closure for its appalling conditions; since then, more "natural" habitats have been created, starting with the Chimps of Mahale Mountains reserve, the Campo Gorilla Exhibit and the Sea Life Cliffs. The program is ongoing, with the Rainforest of the Americas due to open in 2012.

✚ K3 ✉ 5333 Zoo Drive, Griffith Park ☎ 323/644 4200 🕐 Daily 10–5. Closed Christmas 🚌 96 ⅗ Very good 💰 Moderate

Celebrating Americans of Japanese ancestry, the Japanese American National Museum

Kodak Theatre, home to the Academy Awards

MULHOLLAND DRIVE

This winding mountain road with terrific views runs from Hollywood west past Malibu (with an unpaved section closed to vehicles in Topanga State Park). Access to the eastern section is off US101/ Hollywood Freeway; to the western section from Highway 27/ Topanga Canyon Boulevard.

➕ D4–H4

MUSEUM OF TOLERANCE

www.museumoftolerance.com

Opened in 1993, less than a year after the LA riots, the Museum of Tolerance focuses its attentions on both the dynamics of prejudice and racism in America, and the history of the Holocaust. High-tech interactive and experiential exhibits offer a challenging insight into the affects of bigotry. World War II artifacts and documents on the second floor provide the most moving memorial of all.

➕ F6 ✉ Simon Wiesenthal Plaza, 9786 W. Pico Boulevard ☎ 310/772-2505 🕐 Mon–Fri 10–5, Sun 11–5 (Nov–Mar Fri until 3.30). Closed Jewish hols 🚌 SM7, 13

♿ Very good 💲 Moderate ❓ Photo ID needed for admission; reservations recommended

OVIATT BUILDING

www.laconservancy.org

Constructed in 1927, this building was the first in Los Angeles to be designed in the art-deco style. Haberdasher James Oviatt commissioned top European designers to model the building after designs he had seen at the 1925 Paris Exposition.

➕ L6 ✉ 617 S. Olive Street ☎ LA Conservancy tour: 213/430-4219 🚌 DASH B, E 💲 Free, tour moderate

PACIFIC ASIA MUSEUM

www.pacificasiamuseum.org

The eclectic Imperial Chinese-style mansion of Grace Nicholson, an early 20th-century Pasadena art collector and adventurous globe-trotter, harbors LA's premier Asian and Pacific Islands art collections. Start by the koi pond and classical Chinese garden in the courtyard, then move through galleries of prized paintings, prints, sculptures

Views from Runyon Canyon Park along Mulholland Drive

Art-deco design displayed at the Oviatt Building

MORE TO SEE

and ceramics from centuries past.
✚ P3 ✉ 46 N. Los Robles Avenue,
Pasadena ☎ 626/449-2742 🕐 Wed–Sun
10–6. Closed national hols 🚇 Memorial
Park 🚌 780; ARTS 10 💷 Moderate

PALEY CENTER FOR MEDIA
www.paleycenter.org
This tribute to more than 90
years of home entertainment
investigates aspects of broad-
casting from news to *Star Trek*
make-up. Check online schedules
of what's screening in the theater
today, or inquire at the front desk
about individual screening rooms.
✚ F6 ✉ 465 N. Beverly Drive, Beverly
Hills ☎ 310/786-1000 🕐 Wed–Sun 12–5
🚌 4, 704 ⚑ Very good 💷 Moderate

PETERSEN AUTOMOTIVE MUSEUM
www.petersen.org
Displaying more than the requisite
classic cars, this museum traces
the automobile's evolution, along
with celebrity cruisers and the
physics behind motor cars and
driving. This is the largest museum
of its type in the US.

✚ H6 ✉ 6060 Wilshire Boulevard, Mid-
City ☎ 323/930-2277 🕐 Tue–Sun 10–6.
Closed national hols 🚌 DASH Fairfax, 20,
217, 720, 780 ⚑ Very good 💷 Moderate

RICHARD J. RIORDAN CENTRAL LIBRARY
www.lapl.org
This 1926 Beaux Arts treasure is
ornamented with carved reliefs of
great thinkers, writers, scientists
and choice *bons mots*. Check out
the art gallery, public readings and
conversations with authors.
✚ L6 ✉ 630 W. 5th Street ☎ 213/228-
7000 🕐 Tue, Thu 10–8, Wed, Fri–Sat
10–5.30. Tours Tue–Fri 12.30, Sat 11 and 2
🚇 Pershing Square 🚌 DASH A, B, F
💷 Free

SKIRBALL CULTURAL CENTER
www.skirball.org
This spacious museum near
the Getty Center explores the
relationship between 4,000 years
of Jewish culture and modern life
in America. There is an interactive
exhibit for children inspired by the
tale of Noah's Ark. A full calendar
of events includes live music,

A nuclear-powered car at the Petersen Automotive Museum
Noahs Ark Gallery, Skirball Cultural Center

theater, films, lectures and classes.
🕀 D4 ✉ 2701 N. Sepulveda Boulevard
☎ 310/440-4500 🕘 Tue–Fri 12–5,
Sat–Sun 10–5. Closed Jewish and national
hols 🚌 761 💲 Moderate (free Thu)

TOPANGA CANYON
www.parks.ca.gov
Covering more than 11,000 acres
(4,450ha), the state park is a great
place to go hiking. Topanga Creek
runs through the canyon, a scenic
part of the park that became
popular with artists and hippies
since *Waltons* actor Will Geer set
up his Theatricum Botanicum here
in the 1950s.
🕀 A5–B6 ✉ Topanga Canyon Boulevard
west of Pacific Palisades, east of Malibu
🕘 Daily 8am–dusk 💲 Park entry moderate

UNION STATION
With a Spanish Mission Revival-
style design by J. and D. Parkinson,
the station was built by the railroad
companies in 1939. View the lofty,
barrel-shaped ceiling, art-deco
lights and Moorish tile trim of the
main hall.
🕀 L6 ✉ 800 N. Alameda Street ☎ LA

Conservancy tour 213/430-4219 🚇 Union
Station 🚌 DASH B, D 💲 Tour moderate

VIRGINIA ROBINSON MANSION AND GARDENS
www.robinsongardens.org
The late society hostess Virginia
Robinson's Mediterranean-style
villa is set in 6.2 acres (2.5ha) of
lush gardens and groves with
palms, terraces and water features.
🕀 F5 ✉ 1008 Elden Way, Beverly Hills
☎ 310/550-2065 🕘 Tue–Fri 10am and
1pm (by reservation only) 🚌 2, 302
💲 Moderate

WARNER BROTHERS STUDIO VIP TOUR
www.https://vipstudiotour.warnerbros.com
A behind-the-scenes tour for the
serious movie buff. Small groups
(reservations advised; no children
under 8) tour backlot sets, watch
productions in progress and learn
about the craft of movie-making.
🕀 H3 ✉ 3400 W. Riverside Drive, Burbank
☎ 818/972-8687 🕘 Every 20 min
Mon–Fri 8.20–4; extended hours in summer
🚌 222 ♿ Few 💲 Expensive ❓ Photo ID
needed for admission

Union Station entrance, complete with bell tower

Visitors exploring the Virginia Robinson gardens

Further Afield

BOWERS MUSEUM

Top-notch traveling exhibitions complement an outstanding collection of global art and history. There's a nearby "Kidseum" for little ones to explore, too.

➕ Off map, southeast ✉ 2002 N. Main Street, Santa Ana ☎ 714/567-3600 ⏰ Tue–Sun 10–4 🍽 Tangata restaurant (reservations 714/550-0906) 🚇 Santa Ana ✋ Expensive (free 1st Sun of month)

KNOTT'S BERRY FARM

www.knotts.com

At SoCal's original theme park, visit Camp Snoopy and the 1880s frontier Ghost Town, splash around in Wild Water Wilderness or ride a roller coaster. Show up after dark for October's Halloween Haunt, or cool off at Soak City water park next door on hot summer days.

➕ Off map, southeast ✉ 8039 Beach Boulevard, Buena Park ☎ 714/220-5200 ⏰ Call for schedules 🚌 460 ✋ Expensive

LOS ANGELES MARITIME MUSEUM

www.lamaritimemuseum.org

The largest maritime museum on the Pacific coast overlooks the busy Port of Los Angeles. There are dozens of beautifully crafted model ships, art, seafaring relics and real ships to visit.

➕ Off map, south ✉ Berth 84 (at foot of 6th Street), San Pedro ☎ 310/548-7618 ⏰ Tue–Sun 10–5 🚌 447 ✋ Inexpensive

MANHATTAN BEACH

www.ci.manhattan-beach.ca.us

This fashionable beach suburb with cafés along the seafront has good swimming, surfing, beach volleyball and a family-friendly aquarium on the pier.

➕ Off map, south ✉ Manhattan Beach Boulevard (off Hwy 1/Sepulveda Boulevard) 🚇 Metro Green Line 🚌 126; BCT 109

REDONDO BEACH

www.redondobeachresort.org

Redondo is a hotel-lined beach with good swimming and a heated lagoon for children. There is fishing from the pier, sailing, kayaking and winter whale-watching cruises.

➕ Off map, south ✉ Off Pacific Coast Highway (Hwy 1) 🚇 Metro Green Line 🚌 232; BCT 109

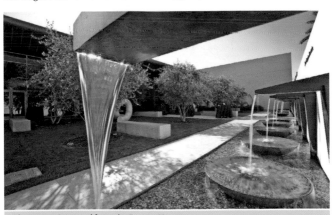

The Huang Courtyard fountain, Bowers Museum

Excursions

CHANNEL ISLANDS

Just off the mainland, Southern California's Channel Islands feel more remote than they are. As early as 12,000 years ago, Native American Chumash tribespeople voyaged to the islands in redwood canoes (called *tomols*) and established villages. In more modern times, Spanish explorers, American ranchers and pioneers, contemporary scientists and holidaymaking pleasure seekers have dropped anchor here.

Civilized Catalina Island is just an hour's ferry ride from the LA ports of Marina del Rey or Long Beach. On Catalina, the main harbor town of Avalon is flooded with day-trippers, especially on weekends and in summer. Stroll by the gloriously restored 1929 art-deco casino, now a movie theater and performance space (tours daily), and through the botanical gardens with bay views. Tour operators lead outdoor trips around the island—anything from kayaking, parasailing and scuba diving to hiking, zip-lining and safari bus rides into the backcountry.

More serene, the Channel Islands National Park protects five islands off the Ventura County coast, north of LA. With over 140 species of plants and animals found nowhere else in the world, this national park's nickname is "California's Galapagos." Native wildlife, including elephant seals, sea lions, bald eagles and Torrey pine trees, is flourishing. The easiest way to visit the park is on a day trip to Anacapa Island; boats depart from Ventura and Oxnard. Multiday guided kayaking, diving, camping and hiking tours are also popular (book ahead).

Distance: 22 miles (35km)
Journey Time: 1–1.5 hours
🚢 Avalon
🛈 No. 1 Green Pier, Santa Catalina, tel 310/510-1520; www.catalinachamber.com
Discovery Tours
☎ 800/626-1496; www.visitcatalinaisland.com
NPS Visitor Center
✉ 1901 Spinnaker Drive, Ventura
☎ 805/658-5730 🕒 Daily 8.30–5

View along the coast at West Anacapa Island
A lighthouse stands in an isolated spot on East Anacapa Island

ORANGE COUNTY BEACHES

Embodying the Southern California lifestyle glimpsed on TV and the silver screen, Orange County offers 42 miles (68km) of sun-kissed beaches alongside the Pacific Coast Highway (Hwy 1). Beach season peaks in July and August.

Orange County's surfing scene revolves around Huntington Beach, nicknamed "Surf City USA." Play beach volleyball on sunny days, then stick around after dark to build a bonfire on the sand. The US Open of Surfing in late summer attracts world-class champions. Downtown is filled with boisterous restaurants, bars and shops.

Posh Newport Beach has its yacht harbor and manicured white-sand beaches. Rent a bicycle and cruise its 4-mile-long (6.4km) Balboa Peninsula, where hotels, cafés and beaches stretch between two piers. Carnival rides await by the 1905 Balboa Pavilion, or catch a short ferry ride over to Balboa Island for more shopping and strolling.

Laguna Beach, an early 20th-century artists' colony further south, has dozens of idyllic beaches along its coastline. In downtown's village, boutiques, art galleries and restaurants nestle inside California bungalows. In July and August, huge crowds show up for the Festival of Arts and the Pageant of the Masters, during which actors dramatically re-create scenes from famous paintings.

Inland, Mission San Juan Capistrano is one of the best-restored and most fetching of California's historic Spanish colonial missions—well worth a detour.

Distance: 60 miles (97km)
Journey Time: 2–3 hours
☒ John Wayne Airport
🔘 Pier Plaza, Pacific Coast Highway (Hwy 1), Huntington Beach, tel 800/729-6232; www.surfcityusa.com
Mission San Juan Capistrano
☎ 26801 Ortega Highway, San Juan Capistrano ☎ 949/234-1300; www.missionsjc.com ☎ Daily 8.30–5. Closed Thanksgiving, Christmas and some rainy days (call ahead)

Golden sands line the coast around Laguna Beach

Surf's up at Huntington Beach

PALM SPRINGS

www.visitpalmsprings.com

Famous for its many golf courses and hot nightlife, Palm Springs is "America's desert playground." Even if you don't play golf, there's plenty to do, from high-end shopping and luxurious spas to horseback riding and hikes to desert-palm oases.

Palm Springs has a fine collection of modernist buildings and great shopping including cutting-edge fashion. Every Thursday evening Villagefest is a free downtown street fair with live music, food and craft vendors, art gallery shows and more. The action is along Palm Canyon Drive, lined with restaurants, cafés, shops, bars and entertainment venues. Nearby, the Palm Springs Art Museum specializes in modern and contemporary artworks, including some by Southern Californians.

For families there's Knott's Soak City, with waterslides, "beaches" and a wave pool for surfing. Then visit The Living Desert zoo and botanical gardens in Palm Desert, where children can walk through a wildlife rehabilitation hospital and take a mini African safari.

If you want to explore the wilderness, try hiking in the Indian Canyons or take the Palm Springs Aerial Tramway up to the top of Mount San Jacinto (8,516ft/ 2,596m). The cars rotate on the way up to give you panoramic views. Joshua Tree National Park, 38 miles (62km) away, is an incredible place to explore the ecology of the Colorado and Mojave deserts.

Distance: 120 miles (193km)
Journey Time: 2–3 hours
✈ Palm Springs Regional Airport
🛈 2901 N. Palm Canyon Drive, tel 760/778-8418 or 800/347-7746, daily 9–5

Knott's Soak City
✉ 1500 S. Gene Autry Trail ☎ 760/327-0499; www.knotts.com 🕒 Jun–Aug daily; Mar–Oct Sat–Sun (call for schedules)

The Living Desert
✉ 47900 Portolo Avenue, ☎ 760/345-5694; www.livingdesert.org 🕒 Daily 9–5 (Jun–Aug 8am–1pm)

The Aerial Tramway climbs to the top of Mount San Jacinto

SANTA BARBARA

www.santabarbaraca.com

Santa Barbara, lying on the coast north of Los Angeles, bills itself as the "American Riviera." Its charming and compact Mediterranean-style downtown and waterfront parks have a lot to offer, from museums to beaches.

In 1925, Santa Barbara was destroyed by an earthquake and subsequently rebuilt in Spanish Mediterranean style. The resulting commercial district is a pleasing harmonious medley of adobe walls, rounded archways, glazed tilework and tile roofs. The waterfront tourist information center can recommend walks that take you past the most historic buildings, including the county courthouse, which features a clock tower observation deck and second-floor Mural Room (guided tours Mon–Sat). Dowtown's art museum houses an excellent collection, including works by Matisse and Chagall, while uptown the graceful Santa Barbara Mission is in an elevated position with views over the city and the ocean.

The waterfront has pleasant parks and vast sandy beaches. Walk out onto rickety wooden Stearns Wharf, dating from 1872, the oldest continuously operating wharf on the US West Coast. Young kids can touch tide-pool critters and come face-to-face with aquarium fish at the wharf's Ty Warner Sea Center. Near the wharf, bicycles and four-wheeled surreys can be rented for pedaling a 3-mile (4.8km) beachfront recreational path, which passes by attractive white strands for swimming, beach volleyball and sunbathing, as well as a bird refuge and small zoo.

Distance: 95 miles (153km)
Journey Time: 2–2.5 hours
⊠ Santa Barbara
🛈 1 Garden Street, tel 805/884-1475, Thu–Tue 9–5
Santa Barbara Museum of Art
⊠ 1130 State Street ☎ 805/963-4364; www.sbmuseart.org ⏰ Tue–Sun 11–5
Santa Barbara Mission
⊠ 2201 Laguna Street ☎ 805/682-4713; www.sbmission.org ⏰ Daily 9–5

County courthouse in Santa Barbara

Looking out over tiled roofs and adobe walls synonymous with Santa Barbara

City Tours

This section contains self-guided tours that will help you explore the sights in each of the city's regions. Each tour is designed to take one or two days, with a map pinpointing the recommended places along the way. There is a quick reference guide at the end of each tour, listing everything you need in that region, so you know exactly what's close by.

Beverly Hills to Hollywood

Hollywood's star is on the rise again. With glamorous shopping, swanky hotels, worthy museums and plenty of celebrity glitz, there's something for all ages and tastes here.

Morning
Get to LA's **Original Farmers' Market** (▷ 116) before the crowds to enjoy an open-air breakfast. Walk south to Mid-City's "Museum Row." If you've got young children in tow, visit the prehistoric **La Brea Tar Pits and Page Museum** (▷ 38–39). Otherwise, make your morning's destination the expanded **Los Angeles County Museum of Art** (▷ 46–47), the biggest art museum in the Western US. Across Wilshire Boulevard, the **Petersen Automotive Museum** (▷ 71) is a homage to LA's car culture.

Mid-morning
Hop on a bus or grab a taxi to **Beverly Hills** (▷ 16–17), where old Hollywood stars built their mansions. The 90210 zip code signals the abode of the rich and famous, who lunch and shop in the "Golden Triangle." Take a trolley tour around town, shop on **Rodeo Drive** (▷ 121) and see what's on at the **Paley Center for Media** (▷ 71).

Lunch
Beverly Hills offers opportunities for star-spotting galore, especially at celebrity-favored restaurants like **Spago Beverly Hills** (▷ 149), **Mr. Chow** (▷ 147) and **Barney Greengrass** (▷ 142). For the best chance of seeing famous faces, book a table at **The Ivy** (▷ 144), a short bus or taxi ride away on Robertson Boulevard, another power-shopping street.

Afternoon

Make a beeline to **Hollywood Boulevard** (▷ 34–35) by bus or taxi. Find your favorite star outside **Mann's Chinese Theatre** (on the Hollywood Walk of Fame). Peek inside the **Kodak Theater** (▷ 69) at the **Hollywood and Highland** center (▷ 118), which offers a perfect photo-op of the Hollywood sign. Inspect movie-making memorabilia at the **Hollywood Museum** (▷ 68–69), then catch a short documentary film about Hollywood's history at the art-deco **Egyptian Theatre** (▷ 67–68). Off the beaten path, **Hollywood Forever** (▷ 68) cemetery surprisingly welcomes camera-toting tourists.

Mid-afternoon

Got energy left to burn? Hop on the Metro Rail and catch a shuttle bus to **Universal Studios Hollywood** (▷ 60–61)—but because theme-park tickets are so expensive, it's best to save this attraction for another full day. Otherwise, it's free to drive up to **Griffith Park** (▷ 32–33), the USA's largest municipal green space, where you'll find the **Griffith Observatory** (▷ 32–33), **Los Angeles Zoo** (▷ 69) and **Autry National Center–Museum of the American West** (▷ 66). If want more shopping this afternoon, catch a bus or taxi down to **Melrose Avenue** (▷ 48–49) for a Mid-City shopping spree.

Evening

West Hollywood has a wealth of glamorous dining rooms for dinner. For something no-fuss, head for **Greenblatt's** deli (▷ 144). It's a convenient launching pad for nights out on the Sunset Strip, hopping between legendary nightclubs such as the **Roxy Theatre** (▷ 135), **Whisky a Go Go** (▷ 137) and the **Comedy Store** (▷ 131). For a more laid-back scene, pack a picnic and attend an outdoor summer concert at the **Hollywood Bowl** (▷ 132).

CITY TOURS

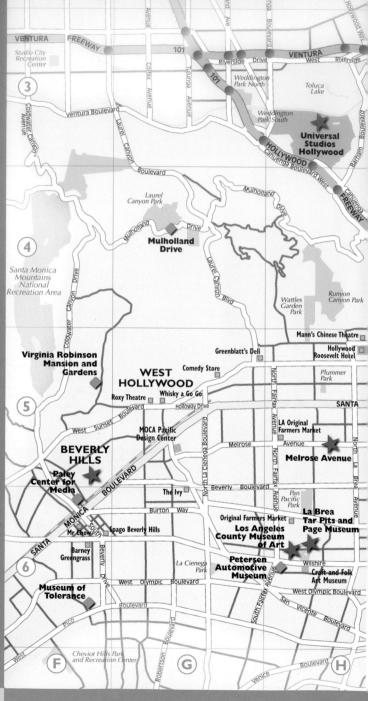

Studio City
Recreation
Center

(3)

VENTURA FREEWAY

101

VENTURA

Riverside Drive

West Riverside

Weddington
Park North

Toluca
Lake

Ventura Boulevard

Weddington
Park South

HOLLYWOOD
Cahuenga Boulevard West

**Universal
Studios
Hollywood**

FREEWAY

Cahuenga Boulevard

Boulevard

Mulholland Drive

**Mulholland
Drive**

(4)

Santa Monica
Mountains
National
Recreation Area

Laurel
Canyon Park

Laurel Canyon Blvd

Wattles
Garden
Park

Runyon
Canyon Park

Mann's Chinese Theatre

Greenblatt's Deli

Hollywood
Roosevelt Hotel

**Virginia Robinson
Mansion and
Gardens**

**WEST
HOLLYWOOD**

Comedy Store

Plummer
Park

SANTA

(5)

Roxy Theatre

Whisky a Go Go

Holloway Drive

West Sunset Boulevard

LA Original
Farmers Market

**BEVERLY
HILLS**

MOCA Pacific
Design Center

Melrose Avenue

Melrose Avenue

**Paley
Center for
Media**

BOULEVARD

The Ivy

Beverly Boulevard

Pan
Pacific
Park

La Brea
Tar Pits and
Page Museum

Burton Way

MONICA

Original Farmers Market

**La Brea
Tar Pits and
Page Museum**

Mr Chow

Spago Beverly Hills

**Los Angeles
County Museum
of Art**

SANTA

Barney
Greengrass

**Petersen
Automotive
Museum**

Craft and Folk
Art Museum

(6)

La Cienega
Park

Wilshire

**Museum of
Tolerance**

West Olympic Boulevard

West Olympic Boulevard

San Vicente Boulevard

Boulevard

PICO

WEST

Cheviot Hills Park
and Recreation Center

(F)

(G)

(H)

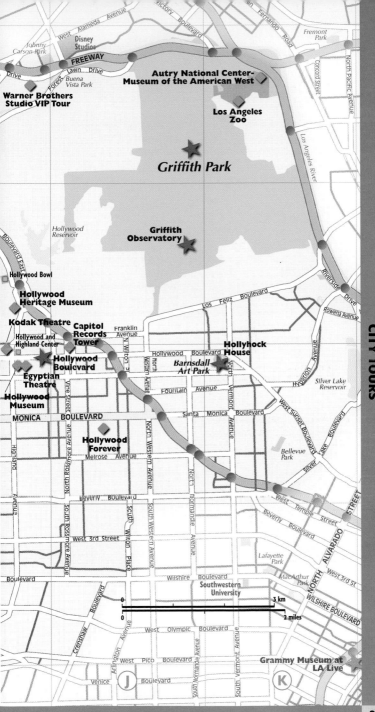

West Alameda Avenue
VICTORY BOULEVARD
San Fernando Road
Fremont Park
Johnny Carson Park
Disney Studios
FREEWAY
Forest Lawn Drive
Buena Vista Park
Drive
Warner Brothers Studio VIP Tour
Autry National Center-Museum of the American West
Los Angeles Zoo
North Pacific Avenue
Concord Street

Griffith Park

Los Angeles River

Hollywood Reservoir
Griffith Observatory
Boulevard East
Riverside Drive
Hollywood Bowl
Hollywood Heritage Museum
Kodak Theatre
Capitol Records Tower
Franklin Avenue
Los Feliz Boulevard
Rowena Avenue
Hollywood and Highland Center
Hollywood Boulevard
N. Wilton
North Western Avenue
Hollywood Boulevard
Barnsdall Art Park
Hollyhock House
Hyperion Avenue
Silver Lake Reservoir
Egyptian Theatre
Vine Street
Fountain Avenue
Hollywood Museum
MONICA BOULEVARD
Santa Monica Boulevard
North Vermont Avenue
West Sunset Boulevard
Highland Avenue
North Rossmore Avenue
Hollywood Forever
Melrose Avenue
North Western Avenue
North Normandie Avenue
Bellevue Park
Silver Lake Boulevard
South Rossmore Avenue
Beverly Boulevard
West Temple Street
North Alvarado Street
West 3rd Street
South Wilton Place
South Western Avenue
Beverly Boulevard
West 3rd St
Lafayette Park
MacArthur Park
Boulevard
Wilshire Boulevard
Southwestern University
WILSHIRE BOULEVARD

0   3 km
0   2 miles

Crenshaw Boulevard
Arlington Avenue
West Olympic Boulevard
South Normandie Avenue
South Vermont Avenue
West Pico Boulevard
Venice J Boulevard
Grammy Museum at LA Live
K

83

Beverly Hills to Hollywood
Quick Reference Guide

CITY TOURS

Barnsdall Art Park and Hollyhock House (▷ 14)
Tour this hilltop home designed by architect Frank Lloyd Wright and enjoy some of the finest views over Hollywood.

Beverly Hills (▷ 16)
Mingle with the rich and famous in LA's most exclusive zip code and then let your credit card run wild on Rodeo Drive.

Griffith Park and Observatory (▷ 32)
The city's largest park is filled with outdoor fun for all the family, plus a zoo, museum and planetarium.

Hollywood Boulevard (▷ 34)
See where the legends began and witness an urban revival of glitz and glam, while you walk in the footsteps of Hollywood's greatest.

La Brea Tar Pits and Page Museum (▷ 38)
This famous fossil site helps you visualize when woolly mammoths once stalked LA's streets.

Los Angeles County Museum of Art (▷ 46)
An awe-inspiring museum campus with global treasures covering almost every aspect of art.

Melrose Avenue and Mid-City Shopping Spree (▷ 48)
For a real shopping experience, browse cutting-edge designers and eclectic hidden boutiques.

Universal Studios Hollywood (▷ 60)
Be transported into the wonderful world of your favorite cartoon characters at LA's movie-making theme park.

MORE TO SEE	64

Autry National Center–Museum of the American West
Capitol Records Tower
Egyptian Theatre
Hollywood Forever
Hollywood Heritage Museum
Hollywood Museum
Kodak Theatre
Los Angeles Zoo

Mulholland Drive
Museum of Tolerance
Paley Center for Media
Petersen Automotive Museum
Virginia Robinson Mansion and Gardens
Warner Brothers Studio VIP Tour

CITY TOURS

85

Downtown

Downtown LA has been revitalized by the heralded construction of Walt Disney Concert Hall and L.A. Live entertainment complex. Historic neighborhoods continue to thrive, with ethnically diverse communities that let visitors take a trip around the world in a day.

Morning

You've got a lot to see today, so fuel up first with a hearty breakfast at the **Original Pantry Café** (▷ 147). Start your explorations where the city began at **El Pueblo de Los Angeles** (▷ 20–21). Wander **Olvera Street** and take a guided historical walking tour. If it's Sunday, mariachi bands may be performing on the plaza.

Mid-morning

Walk south and take a break at **Union Station** (▷ 72); note the art-deco style of the grand waiting-room concourse. Head south to 1st Street, turning right into **Little Tokyo** (▷ 42–43). This Japanese immigrant neighborhood covers just a few blocks, anchored by the **Japanese American National Museum** (▷ 69) and **Geffen Contemporary** (▷ 51) art gallery. Stop by **Fugetsu-do** bakery (▷ 117) for a traditional Japanese snack.

Lunch

Walk or take a bus over to LA's **Grand Central Market** (▷ 30–31). Open for almost a century, this maze of grocery stalls and food vendors is fun just to wander. Alternatively, near Olvera Street, **Philippe the Original** (▷ 148) is an old-fashioned LA institution that claims to have invented the French dip sandwich—taste it for yourself. Or head north to Chinatown for a dim-sum lunch at **Empress Pavilion** (▷ 144).

Afternoon

Atop Grand Avenue, and accessible by bus, the **Museum of Contemporary Art** (▷ 50–51) is a kaleidoscopic experience of art in all media that hosts frequently changing exhibitions. Alternatively, ride the Metro Rail or take a bus south to the **Natural History Museum of LA County** (▷ 52–53)—don't miss the newly reopened Dinosaur Hall. Expo Park's **California Science Center** (▷ 66–67) is also great for entertaining kids.

Dinner

Make sure you've booked a table in advance to dine at **Patina** (▷ 147–148), from star chef Joachim Splichal, or the **Water Grill** (▷ 149), specializing in fresh seafood. Downtown's **L.A. Live** (▷ 29) has outposts of many other famous LA restaurants—sushi bars, steak houses and California farm-to-table eateries. At L.A. Live, you can tour the **GRAMMY Museum** (▷ 28–29), which offers discounted admission after 6pm on nights when special public programs are held.

CITY TOURS

Evening

Sports fans need look no further than the **Staples Center** (▷ 136), also on the L.A. Live campus. For fine arts, head up Grand Avenue for a performance at one of the venues housed in the **Music Center** (▷ 134). If you'd rather not spend big bucks on sports or concert tickets, hopscotch between offbeat bars like **Bordello** (▷ 130), **Golden Gopher** (▷ 131), the **Mayan** (▷ 133) and the **Roof Bar at the Standard Downtown** (▷ 135).

0 ————————— 3 km
0 ————————— 2 miles

4 Hollywood Heritage Museum

Los Feliz Boulevard

Rowena Avenue

Kodak Theatre

Hollywood Boulevard

Franklin Avenue

N. Wilton Avenue

HOLLYWOOD

Hollywood Boulevard

Hollyhock House

Capitol Records Tower

North Western Avenue

FREEWAY

Barnsdall Art Park

North Vermont Avenue

Hyperion Avenue

Silver Lake Reservoir

Egyptian Theatre

Hollywood Museum

Vine Street

Fountain Avenue

West Sunset Boulevard

5 SANTA MONICA BOULEVARD

Santa Monica Avenue

Silver Lake Boulevard

Highland Avenue

North Rossmore Avenue

Hollywood Forever

North Western Avenue

North Normandie Avenue

Santa Monica Boulevard

Bellevue Park

Melrose Avenue

Beverly Boulevard

South Wilton Place

South Western Avenue

West Temple Street

Beverly Boulevard

ALVARADO

West 3rd Street

Wilshire Boulevard

Lafayette Park

MacArthur Park

NORTH

WILSHIRE BOULEVARD

6 South Rossmore Avenue

Crenshaw Boulevard

Arlington Avenue

West Olympic Boulevard

South Normandie Avenue

South Vermont Avenue

Southwestern University

Roof Bar at the Standard

Grammy Museum at LA Live

West Pico Boulevard

Venice Boulevard

Staples Center

West Washington Boulevard

SANTA MONICA FREEWAY

South Normandie Avenue

FREEWAY

7 Adams Blvd

Crenshaw Boulevard

West Jefferson Boulevard

West Jefferson Boulevard

South Hoover Street

HARBOR

East Main Street

Rodeo Road

West 36th Place

University of Southern California

East Jefferson

Exposition Boulevard

Museum of African American Art

Arlington

Natural History Museum of LA County

California Science Center

Exposition Park

East Martin Luther

West Martin Luther King Jr Boulevard

Wilson Field

South Figueroa Street

8 West Vernon Avenue

H

J

K

88

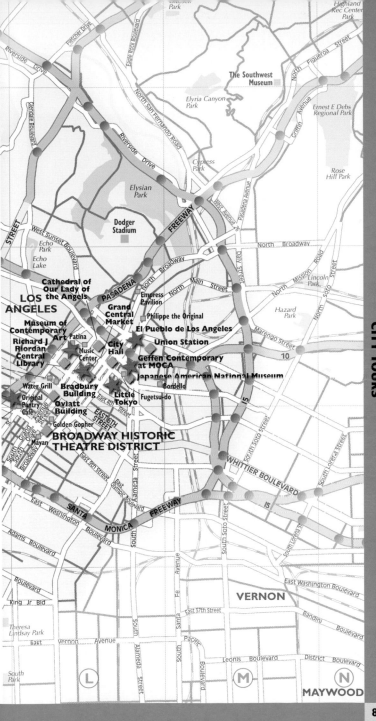

The Southwest Museum

Elyria Canyon Park

Ernest E Debs Regional Park

Rose Hill Park

Dodger Stadium

Elysian Park

Echo Park
Echo Lake

North Broadway

Lincoln Park

Hazard Park

Cathedral of Our Lady of the Angels

LOS ANGELES

PASADENA

Empress Pavilion

Grand Central Market

Philippe the Original

Museum of Contemporary Art

Patina

El Pueblo de Los Angeles

Richard J Riordan Central Library

Music Center

City Hall

Union Station

Geffen Contemporary at MOCA

Japanese American National Museum

Water Grill

Bradbury Building

Little Tokyo

Bordello

Original Pantry Cafe

Oviatt Building

Fugetsu-do

Golden Gopher

EIGHTH STREET

Mayan

BROADWAY HISTORIC THEATRE DISTRICT

WHITTIER BOULEVARD

SANTA MONICA FREEWAY

VERNON

East Washington Boulevard

Adams Boulevard

King Jr Bld

Theresa Lindsay Park

South Park

Vernon Avenue

East 37th Street

Leonis Boulevard

Bandini Boulevard

District Boulevard

L

M

N

MAYWOOD

SIGHTS AND EXPERIENCES

El Pueblo de Los Angeles
(▷ 20)
Standing where the city was founded, this Latin-flavored quarter features a vibrant outdoor market, public plazas and adobe buildings.

GRAMMY Museum at L.A. Live
(▷ 28)
Join the sound revolution while exploring interactive recording studios, a virtual bandstand and recordings by musical stars.

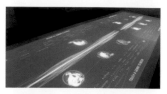

Grand Central Market (▷ 30)
Food vendors at this historic market reflect the city's diverse immigrant cultures. Grand Central Market is near to the landmark Angels Flight Railway.

Little Tokyo (▷ 42)
This Japanese immigrant cultural hub reveals petite gardens, Buddhist temples, noodle shops, sushi bars and an emotionally moving museum.

Museum of Contemporary Art
(▷ 50)
If you have any doubts that LA is a creative capital on a par with New York City, erase them at this archi-tecturally eye-catching museum.

Natural History Museum of LA
County (▷ 52)
Displaying the biggest dinosaurs to the smallest insects, this fun but educational museum takes families on a virtual time-travel trip.

CITY TOURS

CITY TOURS

West LA to Malibu

A mosaic of neighborhoods with idiosyncratic personalities, West LA covers in-vogue Culver City, collegiate Westwood, upper-crust Brentwood and the beach cities of Santa Monica and Venice. Malibu, a star-studded enclave, is a short, but memorably scenic drive north along the Pacific Coast Highway (Hwy 1).

Morning
Rise and shine for breakfast at **Venice Beach** (▷ 62–63). People-watching doesn't get much better than at the **Sidewalk Café** (▷ 148), then join the human circus parading, cycling and in-line skating down Venice's **Ocean Front Walk** (▷ 121). Inland, walk beside the early-20th-century canals that gave Venice its name.

Mid-morning
Browse the art galleries and boutique shops of Venice's **Abbot Kinney Boulevard** (▷ 115) or **Main Street** (▷ 119), further north in Santa Monica. Both shopping districts also have dozens of cafés for a mid-morning snack or espresso break. When you're refreshed, hop on a Big Blue Bus or cycle along the beachside recreational path north to **Santa Monica** (▷ 56–57), LA's biggest and most chic beach city. Work up an appetite strolling Santa Monica Pier, where amusements beckon at **Pacific Park** (▷ 134).

Lunch
High-end dining rooms with ocean views abound in Santa Monica; book a table at **Lobster** (▷ 145) by the pier. Otherwise, just a short walk or bus ride inland, downtown offers more top chefs' restaurants, including **Chinois** (▷ 143) by Wolfgang Puck and the **Border Grill** (▷ 142), from Susan Feniger and Mary Sue Milliken.

Afternoon

Go to the Getty. The only question is, which one? The **Getty Center** (▷ 24–25) is a hilltop museum with a wealth of Western art collections dating from the Middle Ages. North along the PCH, the **Getty Villa** (▷ 26–27) showcases Greek, Roman and Etruscan antiquities in a Mediterranean villa surrounded by peristyle gardens and reflecting pools. If you'd rather browse works by contemporary Southern California artists, take a bus out to **Bergamot Station** (▷ 115), Santa Monica's invigorating art-gallery complex, or the **UCLA Hammer Museum** (▷ 58–59), with progressive art exhibitions in Westwood, near the university's outdoor **Franklin D. Murphy Sculpture Garden** (▷ 68).

Dinner

Head back to the beach in time for sunset, or take a drive up the coastal highway to **Malibu** (▷ 57). For burgers and a beer, hit on the **Father's Office** bar (▷ 144) on **Montana Avenue** (▷ 120), a sleek shopping row just inland from Santa Monica's oceanfront. If you're craving fish for dinner, catch a bus or drive further inland to Brentwood's high-class **Katsuya** sushi bar (▷ 144–145).

Evening

You'll find plentiful bars for hanging out by the beach in both Santa Monica and Venice. If you prefer well-heeled cocktail lounges instead of rowdy dive bars, try **Copa d'Oro** (▷ 131), **Bar Chloe** (▷ 129) or **The Other Room** (▷ 134). Culture vultures can catch a play at the **Geffen Playhouse** (▷ 131) or a concert at **UCLA Live** (▷ 137), both in Westwood. A handful of smaller venues scattered around West LA host more intimate live music shows, including **Harvelle's** blues club (▷ 131) and **McCabe's Guitar Shop** (▷ 133).

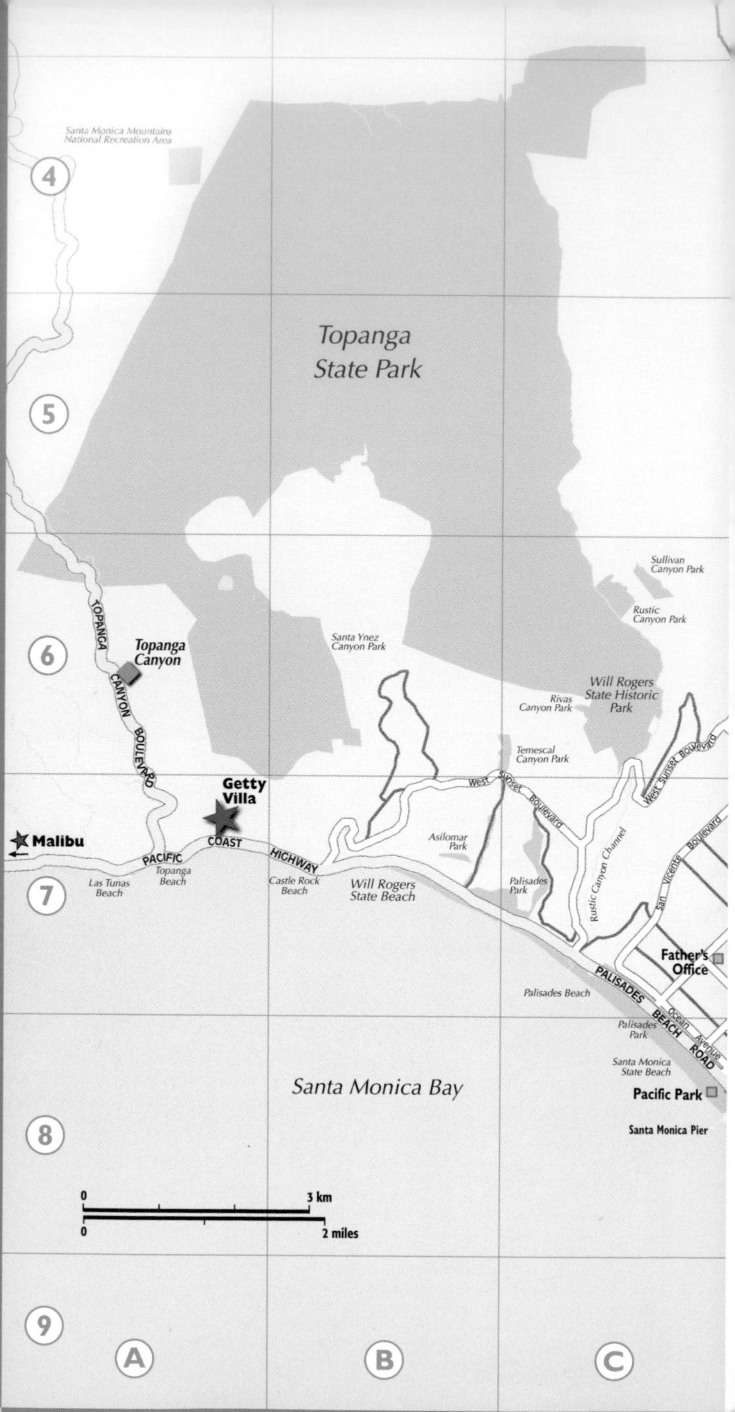

Santa Monica Mountains
National Recreation Area

4

5

Topanga
State Park

TOPANGA CANYON BOULEVARD

6

Topanga
Canyon

Sullivan
Canyon Park

Rustic
Canyon Park

Santa Ynez
Canyon Park

Rivas
Canyon Park

Will Rogers
State Historic
Park

Temescal
Canyon Park

WEST SUNSET BOULEVARD

Getty
Villa

★ Malibu

PACIFIC COAST HIGHWAY

7

Las Tunas
Beach

Topanga
Beach

Castle Rock
Beach

Will Rogers
State Beach

Asilomar
Park

Palisades
Park

Rustic Canyon Channel

SAN VICENTE BOULEVARD

WEST SUNSET BOULEVARD

Father's
Office

PALISADES BEACH ROAD

Palisades Beach

Palisades
Park

Santa Monica
State Beach

Pacific Park

Santa Monica Pier

Santa Monica Bay

8

0   3 km
0   2 miles

9

A   B   C

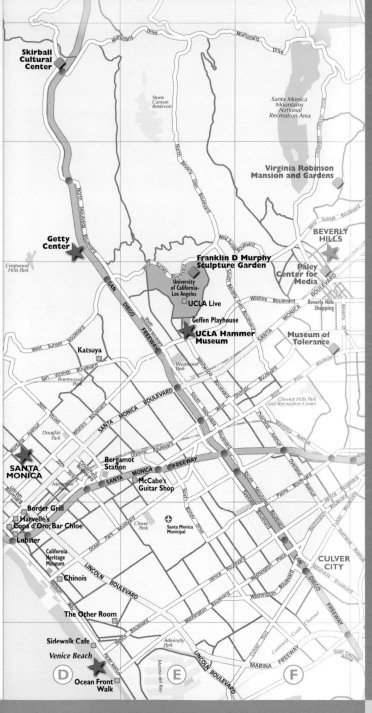

Skirball
Cultural
Center

Stone
Canyon
Reservoir

Mulholland Drive

Mulholland Drive

Santa Monica
Mountains
National
Recreation Area

Virginia Robinson
Mansion and Gardens

West Sunset Boulevard

BEVERLY
HILLS

Getty
Center

Crestwood
Hills Park

Franklin D Murphy
Sculpture Garden

University
of California-
Los Angeles

UCLA Live

Geffen Playhouse

UCLA Hammer
Museum

Paley
Center for
Media

Beverly Hills
Shopping

Wilshire Boulevard

Museum of
Tolerance

Katsuya

West Sunset Boulevard

San Vicente Boulevard

Brentwood
Park

Westwood
Park

Cheviot Hills Park
and Recreation Center

Douglas
Park

Montana Avenue

SANTA
MONICA

Wilshire Boulevard

Bergamot
Station

Olympic Boulevard

McCabe's
Guitar Shop

SANTA MONICA BOULEVARD

SANTA MONICA FREEWAY

Border Grill
Harvelle's
Copa d'Oro; Bar Chloe
Lobster

California
Heritage
Museum

Memorial
Park

Clover
Park

Santa Monica
Municipal

CULVER
CITY

Chinois

LINCOLN BOULEVARD

Venice Boulevard

Washington Boulevard

Washington Boulevard

The Other Room

SAN DIEGO FREEWAY

Sidewalk Cafe

Venice Beach

Admiralty
Park

Centinela Creek Channel

MARINA FREEWAY

LINCOLN BOULEVARD

Ocean Front
Walk

Marina del Rey

D

E

F

95

SIGHTS AND EXPERIENCES

Getty Center (▷ 24)
World-class Western art combines with sublime architecture and stunning panoramic views at the Getty Center, perched looking out over the city.

Getty Villa (▷ 26)
This is the original Getty, where Greek and Roman antiquities are displayed in stunning surroundings at a Mediterranean estate with perfectly manicured gardens.

Santa Monica and Malibu (▷ 56)
Join sun worshippers and surfers at LA's chic beach towns—bustling Santa Monica, or the quieter and more remote Malibu.

UCLA Hammer Museum (▷ 58)
It may not be on the grand scale of some other LA museums, but this lynchpin of the city's contemporary arts scene has impressive European and American art.

Venice Beach (▷ 62)
Wacky and wild, this is the place to hang out doing what ever takes your fancy—strolling the boardwalk, people-watching, volleyball on the beach, or whatever.

MORE TO SEE	64

Franklin D. Murphy Sculpture Garden
Skirball Cultural Center
Topanga Canyon

Pasadena

A cultural hub northeast of Downtown LA, Pasadena possesses world-class museums, sumptuous gardens and plenty of shopping, from antiques markets to chic boutiques. Every January, the Rose Bowl college football game and equally famous Tournament of Roses parade draw enormous crowds.

Morning
Sleep in at your hotel, maybe order room service. There's no need to rush to get to Pasadena early in the morning, because its major sights and attractions open later in the day. If you have a car, drive out to **The Langham Huntington Hotel & Spa** (▷ 158) for a posh breakfast or deluxe Sunday brunch spread.

Mid-morning
On the way, stop by the **Gamble House** (▷ 22–23) to pick up tickets for a guided afternoon tour of LA's Arts and Crafts-style bungalow. Tours sometimes sell out, so it's worth showing up as soon as the visitor center bookstore opens to buy tickets.

Lunch
Stroll through **Old Town Pasadena** (▷ 120), where unique boutiques such as **Gold Bug** (▷ 118) rub shoulders with cafés and restaurants. Dine surounded by sleek, urban-chic at **Mi Piace** (▷ 146). For a taste of Mexican cuisine, **Mijares** (▷ 146) is a century-old cantina nearby. Innovative modern Chinese plates await at **Yujean Kang's** (▷ 149), another packed place for lunch in Old Town.

Afternoon
Take your pick of Pasadena's museums for spending the entire afternoon. Architecture fans won't want to miss the **Gamble House** (▷ 98, Mid-morning), while art lovers can get their fill at the **Norton Simon Museum of Art** (▷ 54–55), a short walk or bus ride west of Old Town. Farther east along Colorado Boulevard (frequent buses run in both directions) is the pint-sized **Pacific Asia Museum** (▷ 70–71), another stop for art and culture.

Mid-afternoon
Unwind with a stroll through the gardens of **The Huntington** (▷ 36–37), an early-20th-century estate house with a fine collection of art masterworks from Europe and the Americas, as well as rare library manuscripts. There is no public transportation here, so you'll have to drive or take a taxi. Alternatively, hop on a bus out to the **LA County Arboretum & Botanic Garden** (▷ 40–41), where plants from around the world grow beside historic houses; the arboretum's tram tour speeds along sightseeing.

Dinner
Make reservations for one of Pasadena's well-heeled dining rooms. Downtown standard bearers for California cuisine include the **Parkway Grill** (▷ 147), influenced by the Mediterranean and Asia, and the traditional **Arroyo Chop House** (▷ 142) for steaks and lobster. Or try French fusion **Bistro 45** (▷ 142) on S. Mentor Avenue in the South Lake Avenue shopping district.

Evening
Pasadena isn't known for its nightlife, but several wine bars, pubs and cinemas liven up Old Town after dark. For fine arts, catch a special show at the **Pasadena Civic Auditorium** (▷ 134) or a performance of the **Pasadena Symphony** (▷ 134), which puts on summer pop concerts outdoors at the **Rose Bowl**.

Oak Grove Park

Alta Park

Devils Gate Reservoir

Farnsworth Park

Mount Lowe Park

West Altadena Drive

East Altadena Drive

East

ALTADENA

Oak Grove Drive

Lincoln Avenue

Fair Oaks Avenue

Lake Avenue

West Woodbury Road

East Woodbury Road

Linda Vista Avenue

Arroyo Seco Wash

North Fair Oaks Avenue

710

La Pintoresca Park

North Lake Avenue

East Washington

McDonald Park

North Hill Avenue

Rose Bowl

Brenner Park

Washington Park

Orange Grove Boulevard

East Orange Grove

Villa Park

Jefferson Park

Brookside Park

Gamble House ★

Old Town Pasadena

Norton Simon Museum of Art ★

Mi Piace

Gold Bug

Parkway Grill

Pacific Asia Museum ◆

Colorado

Bistro 45

Grant Park

East Del Mar

Eagle Rock Reservoir

Eagle Rock Recreation Center

Yujean Kang's

Central Park

Pasadena Civic Auditorium

Arroyo Chop House

South Lake Avenue

East

South Arroyo Parkway

North Hill Avenue

Pasadena Symphony

Lower Arroyo Park

Mijares

WEST CALIFORNIA BOULEVARD

South Orange Grove Boulevard

South Fair Oaks Avenue

SOUTH ARROYO PARKWAY

South Los Robles Avenue

Tournament Park

SAN MARINO

North Figueroa Street

Garvanza Park

Arroyo Park

Columbia St.

Langham Huntingdon Hotel & Spa

Garfield Avenue

Lacy Park

Huntington

PASADENA FREEWAY

Arroyo Seco Park

Mission Street

Monterey Road

Fair Oaks Avenue

Garfield Park

North Garfield Avenue

North Atlantic Boulevard

San Pasqual Creek

Stony Park

Ernest E. Debs Regional Park

El Sereno North Park

SOUTH PASADENA

Alhambra Park

West Main Street

South Fremont Avenue

Rose Hill Park

Huntington Drive North

Ⓝ

Ⓟ

West Mission Road

South Garfield Avenue

East

Altadena Drive

North Altadena Drive

Eaton Canyon Creek

Eaton Canyon Park

Sierra Madre Reservoir

New York Drive

Eaton Canyon Reservoir

Hamilton Park

SIERRA MADRE

Boulevard

Victory Park

Sunnyslope Park

West Sierra Madre Boulevard

East Sierra Madre Boulevard

Sierra Vista Park

Memorial Park

PASADENA

Boulevard

East Walnut Street

East Foothill Boulevard

West Foothill Boulevard

Colorado Place

Boulevard

East Colorado Boulevard

LA County Arboretum & Botanic Garden

South San Gabriel Boulevard

Eaton Blanche Park

Hugo Reid Park

North Baldwin Avenue

ARCADIA

Boulevard

Macre Boulevard

Sierra

EAST PASADENA

Del Mar Avenue

The Huntington

Botanical Gardens

Huntington Drive

West Huntington Drive

West Duarte Road

South Baldwin Avenue

Drive

North Del Mar Avenue

North San Gabriel Boulevard

Eaton Wash

Rubio Wash

TEMPLE CITY

ROSEMEAD BOULEVARD

EAST SAN GABRIEL

East Las Tunas Drive

Las Tunas Drive

Live Oak Park

Smith Park

Sally Tanner Park

0 _____ 3 km
0 _____ 2 miles

Mission Road

SAN GABRIEL

South Del Mar Avenue

Mission Drive

ROSEMEAD BOULEVARD

Rosemead Park

Baldwin Avenue

Almansor Park

ALHAMBRA

Vincent Lugo Park

East Valley Boulevard

Valley Boulevard

Q   R   S

SIGHTS AND EXPERIENCES

Gamble House (▷ 22)

Considered by some to be the epitome of Southern California's Arts and Crafts bungalow style, this two-story home harmonizes architecture with nature. Learn more on a guided behind-the-scenes tour. More Arts and Crafts historic homes are just a short walk away in this leafy neighborhood.

The Huntington (▷ 36)

Join the high society of Pasadena's early rich-and-famous lifestyles at the former estate of railroad tycoon Henry Huntington. Stroll through the art galleries and library, then delight in high tea among the roses or take a wander through the estate's stunning, meditative landscape gardens.

LA County Arboretum & Botanic Garden (▷ 40)

Exotic public gardens spread across the foothills of the San Gabriel Mountains. Take a walk or hop aboard a tram to tour the expansive grounds, where something is always blooming year-round; nearby are a handful of historic houses.

Norton Simon Museum of Art (▷ 54)

Inspiring paintings and sculptures are the focus of this petite, but nevertheless impressive, art museum focused on Europe and the Americas, from Monet to Matisse, Degas to Diego Rivera. The Asian art collections also play a starring role.

MORE TO SEE

64

Pacific Asia Museum

SHOP

110

Arts and Antiques
Gold Bug
Rose Bowl Flea Market
Books and Music
Canterbury Records
Distant Lands
Vroman's

Shopping Districts
Mission Street
Old Town Pasadena
South Lake Avenue

ENTERTAINMENT

124

Live Music and Performing Arts
Pasadena Civic Auditorium
Pasadena Symphony

Sports and Leisure
Santa Anita Race Track

EAT

138

Asian
Saladang Song
Yujean Kang's
California Cuisine
Parkway Grill
The Raymond
French
Bistro 45

Italian
Mi Piace
Mexican and Southwestern
Mijares
Steak and Seafood
Arroyo Chop House

Cacti in the Desert Garden at The Huntington

Further Afield

Head outside the city center to discover more of LA's favorite playgrounds, from South Bay beach towns and the harborside attractions of Long Beach to the mega-popular Disneyland Resort theme parks in Anaheim, Orange County.

CITY TOURS

DAY 1 Morning

Start your morning with breakfast by the ocean, driving south of LAX airport to **Manhattan Beach** (▷ 73). Learn to surf or play beach volleyball on the sands, then walk out onto the pier to visit the kid-friendly aquarium. Uphill from the beach, busy streets are lined with breezy boutiques, as well as cafés for a mid-morning break or an early lunch. Further south, **Redondo Beach** (▷ 73) offers a fishing pier and swimming in protected, heated lagoons.

Mid-morning

Drive down to **Long Beach** (▷ 44–45) after lunch. Right on the waterfront, the **Aquarium of the Pacific** (▷ 44) is one of the West Coast's biggest aquariums, with marine wildlife exhibits enough to keep the whole family entertained. Hop aboard a water taxi or drive across the harbor to where the *Queen Mary* (▷ 44) is docked. Nautical enthusiasts can take a self-guided audio tour of this historic ocean liner, or join a guided ghost-hunting excursion through the ship's eerie salons and suites after dark.

Evening

The *Queen Mary* is also a functioning hotel with restaurants and bars, if you care to linger overnight. Otherwise, drive east along the shoreline to catch sunset from the beach at **Belmont Shores** or from a floating gondola off **Naples Island**. Both neighborhoods have restaurants and bars to while away an evening.

DAY 2 Morning

It takes at least a full day to experience **Disneyland Resort** (▷ 18–19) in Orange County, accessible by train, bus or car from Downtown LA or LAX airport. Where orange groves once flourished, Walt Disney first "imagineered" his Disneyland theme park in 1955. The ideal place to start your explorations is on Disneyland's Main Street, U.S.A. Classic rides await in the park's themed areas, including the retro-futuristic Tomorrowland, safari-style Adventureland and New Orleans Square, which has the popular Pirates of the Caribbean ride. Younger children will have fun with Mickey's Toontown characters and the gentler rides and attractions of Fantasyland.

Afternoon

With a park hopper ticket, you can also visit **Disney California Adventure** (▷ 19) the same day. A homage to the Golden State's pop culture and natural attractions, this neighboring theme park has its own rides and cartoon-inspired parades. Go virtual hang-gliding in the Golden State area of the park, then ride the California Screamin' roller coaster at Paradise Pier and watch the Pixar Play Parade. Route 66-themed Cars Land is new to this park in 2012, which also offers movie studio-themed attractions and the Tower of Terror ride.

© Disney

Evening

After dark, Disneyland explodes fireworks over Sleeping Beauty Castle and runs the Fantasmic! aquatic lights show. The equally dazzling World of Color show takes place at Paradise Pier inside Disney California Adventure. Just outside the parks, **Downtown Disney** is a popular open-air entertainment complex with shops, restaurants, bars, nightclubs, cinemas and video-game arcades.

CITY TOURS

Sepulveda Dam Recreation Area

Santa Barbara

Bob Hope Airport

GOLDEN STATE FREEWAY

101

134

5

Universal Studios Hollywood

Griffith Park

GLENDALE

2

Santa Monica Mountains National Recreation Area

WEST HOLLYWOOD

405

HOLLYWOOD FREEWAY

5

110

BEVERLY HILLS

University of California

SANTA MONICA BOULEVARD

2

HOLLYWOOD

Elysian Park

SAN DIEGO FREEWAY

SANTA MONICA BOULEVARD

WILSHIRE BOULEVARD

Channel Islands

10

SANTA MONICA FREEWAY

LOS ANGELES

10

University of Southern California

110

Santa Monica Municipal Airport

CULVER CITY

Kenneth Hahn State Recreation Area

SANTA MONICA

7

Venice Beach

Loyola Marymount University

INGLEWOOD

HUNTINGTON PARK

FIRESTONE BOULEVARD

Los Angeles International Airport

LYNWOOD

Dockweiler Beach

105

CENTURY FREEWAY

Manhattan Beach

HAWTHORNE

HARBOR FREEWAY

COMPTON

405

91

ARTESIA FREEWAY

710

REDONDO BEACH

107

SAN DIEGO FREEWAY

TORRANCE

Redondo Beach

1

Torrance Municipal Airport

PACIFIC COAST HIGHWAY

1

110

PALOS VERDES

Long Beach Harbor

San Pedro Channel

Los Angeles Maritime Museum

| 0 | | 10 km |
| 0 | | 6 miles |

210

PASADENA

134

Angeles
National Forest

210

210

Santa Fe Dam
Recreation
Area

605

ALHAMBRA

California
State University
Los Angeles

EL MONTE

BALDWIN
PARK

10

SAN BERNARDINO FREEWAY

**Palm
Springs**

10

60

Whittier
Narrows
Recreation
Area

WHITTIER BOULEVARD

72

Rose Hills
Memorial
Park

60

710

5

19

605

72

WHITTIER

DOWNEY

90

90

105

PARAMOUNT

91

San Gabriel

El Dorado
Park

91

5

5

FULLERTON

91

91

Long Beach
Airport

19

**Knott's
Berry Farm**

CYPRESS

ANAHEIM
**Disneyland®
Resort**

5

405

Rancho Los
Alamitos

GARDEN GROVE

Crystal
Cathedral

22

**LONG
BEACH**

Queen Mary

San Pedro
Bay

Seal Beach
National
Refuge

Seal Beach

WESTMINSTER

SAN DIEGO FREEWAY

**Bowers
Museum**

HUNTINGTON
BEACH

39

Orange County Beaches

NEWPORT
BEACH

55

SIGHTS AND EXPERIENCES

Disneyland Resort (▷ 18)

Far and away the most popular theme park in Southern California, this Orange County mega-attraction takes at least a day to fully experience. It's not just for little kids either—honeymooning couples, grandparents and teens all get a kick out of the cartoon attractions, rides and shows. Arrive early in the morning to beat the crowds, or stay after dark to see the fireworks. Now, with the added bonus of Disney California Adventure, two is better than one.

© Disney

Long Beach and the *Queen Mary* (▷ 44)

South of Downtown LA, Long Beach's major sights, including the Aquarium of the Pacific and the historic *Queen Mary* ocean liner, cluster by the waterfront, making sightseeing by water taxi easy. Come face to snout with the aquarium's many denizens of the deep, such as sharks and seals, then take a guided ghost-hunting tour of the ocean liner's supposedly haunted cabins and decks. Further east, Belmont Shores' beach and the artificial canals of Naples await.

| MORE TO SEE | 64 |

Bowers Museum
Knott's Berry Farm
Los Angeles Maritime Museum
Manhattan Beach
Redondo Beach

CITY TOURS

Shop

Whether you're looking for the best local products, a department store or a quirky boutique, you'll find them all in Los Angeles. In this section shops are listed alphabetically.

SHOP

Introduction

The ultimate purchase, in this city where car is king, may be a custom vehicle; perhaps an impeccably restored Bentley or Excalibur, or a hand-painted, flower-power Volkswagen bus. Still this is not the usual afternoon's shopping spree purchase.

Fashion

In this fashion-conscious (and, occasionally, fashion-victim) city, almost everyone wants to be decked out in trendy clothing and costly jewels, especially if a hip restaurant or nightclub is on the agenda, or a trip past a scrutinizing doorman is in the picture. And as you search among the city's hot boutiques for that special something that will get you from a yoga class to an Oscar party, you may well spot a celebrity or two.

Something from Rodeo Drive (▷ 121) or Melrose Avenue (▷ 48–49) is de rigueur—you'll find everything from mass-produced imports and hard-to-find vintage wear to pricey one-of-a-kind designs and jewelry, cool clubwear, shoes, bags, and other accessories. Not surprisingly, many of these creations come with sky-high price tags, but it's nonetheless possible to waltz out of the door with some bauble or bangle you can actually afford.

Leisure Gear

However, it's not the high life and the beautiful people that draw all visitors to LA; many come for its enviable climate and myriad sports

---

GRAB THE GLITZ

It's probably not a good idea to pry up a cement block of John Wayne's footprints at Mann's Chinese Theatre, like Lucille Ball did in an episode of *I Love Lucy*, but there are plenty of other movie-memorabilia souvenirs available. Hollywood Boulevard is lined with stores that sell movie-related T-shirts, baseball caps, shot glasses, water globes, key chains, posters, coffee mugs and other items.

From the chic streets of Rodeo Drive to the tourist honeypot Hollywood Boulevard, LA is a shopper's

activities. Considering this combination, it's not surprising that sports equipment, surfboards, skateboards, rollerblades and a mind-boggling array of T-shirts, swimsuits, wetsuits, athletic wear and running shoes in a wide range of prices can be found all over town. Tennis and golf gear are also best-sellers, and you will find something suitable for hitting the court or course, whether you play in a public park or a fancy country club.

House and Garden

You will also find a broad selection of quirky and high-end housewares. Angelenos, as fashion conscious about their homes and gardens as they are about their bodies, have assured a brisk business for purveyors of decorative items.

Music

Music is big business in the city. Humongous stores on the Sunset Strip and smaller specialized shops sell a dizzying range of new and used CDs that showcase every type of music, and associated merchandise, available under the sun.

Books

From small shops to big retail chains, bookstores are plentiful here. Some focus on specialized interests such as cinema, cooking or mystery novels, while others offer a variety.

MY BODY IS A TEMPLE

Health- and body-conscious Los Angeles seduces shoppers with a multitude of products to soothe and beautify. Luxury spas and salons, as well as budget shops and flea markets, offer avocado facials, aromatherapy oils, hand-milled soaps and face-lifts in a bottle. This regime, naturally, extends itself to food and drink—natural foods, nutritional supplements and soy bean products are easy to find throughout the region.

paradise, offering everything from designer clothes, shoes and books to items for the home

Directory

Beverly Hills to Hollywood

Art and Antiques
Gemini G.E.L.
Margo Leavin Gallery
Wacko
Wanna Buy A Watch?

Books and Music
Amoeba Music
Bodhi Tree
Book Soup
Larry Edmunds'
  Bookshop

Men's and Women's Clothing
Fred Segal
Frederick's of
  Hollywood
Kitson
Lisa Kline
Maxfield
Space 15 Twenty
Trina Turk

Movie Memorabilia
Samuel French Inc.

Secondhand and Vintage Clothing
American Rag
It's A Wrap
Squaresville
Wasteland

Shopping Districts
Larchmont Boulevard
Rodeo Drive
Sunset Plaza

Shopping Malls
Beverly Center
The Grove
Hollywood and
  Highland
Universal CityWalk

Specialty Shops
Meltdown
Plastica
Soolip Paperie &
  Press

Downtown

Art and Antiques
Cirrus Gallery

Shopping Districts
Chung King Road
Santee Alley

Shopping Malls
Seventh & Fig

Specialty Shops
Flower Market
Fugetsu-do
St. Vincent Jewelry
  Center

West LA to Malibu

Art and Antiques
Bergamot Station
Broadway Gallery
  Complex
Del Mano Gallery
Santa Monica
  Outdoor Antique
  and Collectible
  Market

Books and Music
Every Picture Tells
  a Story
Small World Books

Men's and Women's Clothing
The Blue Jeans Bar
Fred Segal
FrontRunners

Secondhand and Vintage Clothing
Gotta Have It
Paris 1900

Shopping Districts
Abbot Kinney
  Boulevard
Main Street
Montana Avenue
Third Street
  Promenade
Westwood Village

Shopping Malls
Brentwood Gardens
Westfield Century City
Westside Pavilion

Specialty Shops
Compartes
H.D. Buttercup
The Puzzle Zoo

Pasadena

Art and Antiques
Gold Bug
Rose Bowl Flea
  Market

Books and Music
Canterbury Records
Distant Lands
Vroman's

Shopping Districts
Mission Street
Old Town Pasadena
South Lake Avenue

SHOP

Shopping A-Z

ABBOT KINNEY BOULEVARD

The street, named for the founder of Venice California, has a variety of shops, from antique furniture and contemporary galleries to clothing boutiques. It's the place to visit for home furnishings.

⊞ D9 ✉ Abbot Kinney (between Palms Boulevard and Brooks Avenue), Venice Beach 🚌 333; SM1, 2,

AMERICAN RAG

www.amrag.com

Most come here for the high-fashion denim bar and the vintage clothing collection, which covers hippie to grunge, 1970s glam and 1980s unspeakable.

⊞ H6 ✉ 150 S. La Brea, Mid-City ☎ 323/935-3154 🚌 14, 16, 212

AMOEBA MUSIC

www.amoeba.com

This Northern California independent music store has added a southern branch in Hollywood with the same stellar selection of new and used CDs and vinyl LPs. There are occasional free performances.

⊞ J5 ✉ 6400 Sunset Boulevard, Hollywood ☎ 323/245-6400 🚌 2, 302

BERGAMOT STATION

www.bergamotstation.com

This old trolley station now houses more than 35 contemporary galleries dealing in an exciting range of art, sculpture, furniture and glass, as well as photography.

⊞ D7 ✉ 2525 Michigan Avenue, Santa Monica 🚌 SM5

BEVERLY CENTER

www.beverlycenter.com

This major-league mall has around 160 upscale fashion, department and specialty stores, plus cinemas

and a good range of restaurants.

⊞ G6 ✉ 8500 Beverly Boulevard, Mid-City ☎ 310/854-0070 🕐 Mon–Fri 10–9, Sat 10–8, Sun 11–6 🚌 DASH 14, 16, 316

THE BLUE JEANS BAR

www.thebluejeansbar.com

Expect an array of the latest hot denim labels, and willing clerks to help ensure you find the right jeans for your figure.

⊞ D7 ✉ 1409 Montana Avenue, Santa Monica ☎ 310/656-7898 🚌 SM3

BODHI TREE

www.bodhitree.com

This is the New Age bookshop where Shirley MacLaine got metaphysical.

⊞ H5 ✉ 8585 Melrose Avenue, West Hollywood ☎ 310/659-1733 🚌 DASH Fairfax, 10

BOOK SOUP

Book Soup features classics to crime, to reference books and more; the art history and movie sections are also good.

⊞ G5 ✉ 8818 Sunset Boulevard, West Hollywood ☎ 310/659-3110 🚌 2, 302

BRENTWOOD GARDENS

The outdoor Brentwood mall is high-end and relatively small, with three levels of shops and restaurants. The shops sell everything from shoes and clothing to home furnishings.

⊞ D6 ✉ 11677 San Vicente Boulevard, Brentwood 🚌 SM3, 4

BROADWAY GALLERY COMPLEX

This is another Santa Monica arts enclave specializing in contemporary paintings, prints and functional art such as furnishings with a

Spanish Steps, Rodeo Drive

distinctive California style.
➕ D7 ✉ Broadway (between 20th Street and Cloverfield Boulevard), Santa Monica
🚌 704; SM1, 10, 11

CANTERBURY RECORDS
www.canterburyrecords.com
This music shop, in business 55-odd years, specializes in big-band, jazz and classical music.
➕ P3 ✉ 805 E. Colorado Boulevard
☎ 626/792-7184 🚌 181, 780; ARTS 10; FT187

CHUNG KING ROAD
An *L.A. Weekly* art critic called this pedestrian alley LA's East Village. It's loaded with art galleries and also gift shops selling Chinatown souvenirs. The galleries coordinate group art openings.
➕ L6 ✉ Between Yale and Hill streets
🚌 DASH B

CIRRUS GALLERY
www.cirrusgallery.com
Founded in 1971, Cirrus is one of the first art dealers in Downtown, near Little Tokyo and the Geffen Contemporary at MOCA. It exhibits works by new and emerging artists, particularly from the west coast of the US. There's also a range of gifts designed by artists, and a bookstore.
➕ L6 ✉ 542 S. Alameda Street
☎ 213/680-3473 🚌 DASH A

COMPARTES
www.compartes.com
You'll find handmade 1950-style confections here, from truffles to stuffed fruits to "love nuts."
➕ E6 ✉ 912 S. Barrington Avenue, Westwood ☎ 310/ 826-3380 🚌 SM3, 4

DEL MANO GALLERY
www.delmano.com
There's a terrific array of innovative and affordable contemporary crafts ranging from jewelry to art glass, ceramics and furnishings here.
➕ E7 ✉ 2001 Westwood Boulevard, Westwood ☎ 310/441-2001 🚌 SM8, 12

DISTANT LANDS
www.distantlands.com
This complete travelers' bookstore covers the globe with guidebooks, maps, DVDs and CDs, luggage and handy travel accessories.
➕ P3 ✉ 20 S. Raymond Avenue, Pasadena ☎ 626/449-3220 Ⓜ Memorial Park 🚌 ARTS 10; FT187

LA'S ORIGINAL FARMERS' MARKET
Born in the Depression at 6333 W. 3rd Street, Mid-City, when local farmers would bring their produce here to sell, the market has become an LA institution. It's touristy, and tacky souvenirs abound, but you can still find fresh fruit and vegetables, butchers, bakers, deli counters and great-value fast food, from coffee and doughnuts to po'boy sandwiches.

EVERY PICTURE TELLS A STORY

www.everypicture.com

This captivating bookstore-gallery displays original art and lithographs from children's books: Garth Williams, Walt Disney and Maurice Sendak.

🔲 D7 ✉ 1333 Montana Avenue, Santa Monica ☎ 310/451-2700 🚌 SM3

FLOWER MARKET

www.laflowerdistrict.com

Two large buildings make up the Flower Market, in LA's Flower District. Look for basics like roses and tulips, or more unusual plants. It's best to come early if you want a good selection.

🔲 L7 ✉ 766 Wall Street ☎ 213/627-3696 🕐 Mon, Wed, Fri 8am–noon, Tue, Thu, Sat 6am–noon 🚌 DASH D, E

FREDERICK'S OF HOLLYWOOD

www.fredericks.com

Celebrated trashy-chic lingerie, brassieres that enhance "sans surgery," stiletto heels and feather boas can be found here—so kinky it's cool.

🔲 H5 ✉ 6751 Hollywood Boulevard, Hollywood ☎ 323/957-5953 🚇 Hollywood/Highland 🚌 217, 780

FRED SEGAL

www.fredsegal.com

Fred Segal is a legendary and eternally hip Melrose specialty store complex owned by Ron Herman. Sportswear and designer collections for men, women and children feature, but also gifts, accessories, shoes, lingerie and luggage. There's another outpost near the beach, a must-visit shopping destination, both for star sightings.

🔲 G5 ✉ 8100 Melrose Avenue, West

Hollywood ☎ 323/651-4129 🚌 10 🔲 D8 ✉ 420 and 500 Broadway, Santa Monica ☎ 310/394-9814 🚌 SM2, 3, 4, 5, 9

FRONTRUNNERS

www.frontrunnersla.com

LA and exercise go hand in hand, so shop for stylish workout and fitness gear where the locals go.

🔲 D6 ✉ 11620 San Vicente Boulevard, Brentwood ☎ 310/820-7585 🚌 SM3, 4

FUGETSU-DO

www.fugetsu-do.com

This traditional Little Tokyo confectionery shop has baked sweet *mochi* and *manju* (pounded-rice cakes) since 1903.

🔲 L6 ✉ 315 E. First Street, Downtown ☎ 213/625-8595 🚌 DASH A

GEMINI G.E.L.

www.geminigel.com

Prints by top American/US-based 20th-century artists, including Jasper Johns, Robert Rauschenberg, Richard Serra and David Hockney, are stocked here.

🔲 H5 ✉ 8365 Melrose Avenue, West Hollywood ☎ 323/651-0513 🚌 10

GOLD BUG

www.goldbugpasadena.com

This curious Victorian-esque treasure box of art, jewelry and home decor, inspired by the natural world, also stocks romantic women's fashions.

➕ P3 ✉ 22 E. Union Street, Pasadena
☎ 626/744-9963 🚇 Memorial Park
🚌 181, 780; ARTS 10; FT187

GOTTA HAVE IT

www.gottahaveitvenice.com

Behind an eye-catching facade with a playing card design are crowded ranks of wildly assorted retro wear for guys and gals.

➕ D9 ✉ 1516 Pacific Avenue, Venice Beach ☎ 310/392-5949 🚌 SM1, 2

THE GROVE

www.thegrovela.com

Architectural styles range from Italian Renaissance to art-deco at this huge outdoor complex at the farmers' market (▷ 116).

➕ H6 ✉ 189 The Grove Drive, Mid-City
☎ 323/900-8080 🚌 DASH Fairfax, 16, 218, 316, 780

H.D. BUTTERCUP

www.hdbuttercup.com

Here more than 30 manufacturers offer interior design advice on antiques, rugs, linens, cashmere throws and modern furniture.

➕ G7 ✉ 3225 Helms Avenue, Culver City
☎ 310/558-8900 🚌 33, CC1

HOLLYWOOD AND HIGHLAND

www.hollywoodandhighland.com

This five-floor, open-air retail and entertainment complex, has chain establishments, boutiques, eateries, cinemas, the Kodak Theatre (▷ 69) and views of the Hollywood sign.

➕ H5 ✉ Hollywood Boulevard and Highland Avenue, Hollywood ☎ 323/467-6412 🚇 Hollywood/Highland 🚌 DASH Hollywood, 217, 780

IT'S A WRAP

www.itsawraphollywood.com

Movie and television studio wardrobe departments offload their extravagances at this bulging shop. There is a second location at 3315 W. Magnolia Boulevard in Burbank.

➕ G6 ✉ 1164 S. Robertson Boulevard, Mid-City ☎ 310/246-9727 🚌 220; SM5, 7, 12

KITSON

www.shopkitson.com

The trendy, fashionable clothes and accessories found here are popular with LA celebs.

➕ G6 ✉ 115 S. Robertson Boulevard, Beverly Hills ☎ 310/859-2652 🚌 14, 220

LARCHMONT BOULEVARD

Larchmont Village is a shopping district with largely mom and pop shops, including an old-fashioned general store with a toy section that has unusual and well-made

---

DESIGN DISTRICT

The interior design capital of Southern California, West Hollywood has a wealth of art and antiques galleries, plus around 300 design stores and showrooms mainly around the west end of Melrose Avenue and San Vicente Boulevard. Here is the Pacific Design Center (aka "The Blue Whale" for its size and color), which harbors more than 130 showrooms offering furniture, fabrics, lighting and kitchen products. They are open to the general public (Mon–Fri 9–5), though some may require an appointment. Visit www.pacificdesigncenter.com.

toys, a high-end women's clothing store, a bookstore and many good restaurants. Be sure to catch the excellent farmers' market here every Sunday.

➕ J6 ✉ Larchmont Boulevard (between Melrose Avenue and 3rd Street) 🚌 14, 16

LARRY EDMUNDS' BOOKSHOP

www.larryedmunds.com

This small but rich trawling ground for cinematic bibliophiles stocks all sorts of film and theater-related tomes, plus posters and stills.

➕ H5 ✉ 6644 Hollywood Boulevard, Hollywood 📞 323/463-3273 🚌 217

LISA KLINE

www.lisakline.com

For more than a decade, the Robertson branch has been the place to go for the latest fashions and for pieces from up-and-coming designers. The kid's store at No. 123 also carries fashion-forward clothes and accessories.

➕ G6 ✉ 143 S. Robertson Boulevard, Mid-City 📞 310/385-7113 🚌 14, 220

MAIN STREET

www.mainstreetsm.com

Hip boutiques, arty design and novelty shops are helpfully interspersed with the excellent restaurants on Main Street.

➕ D8–D9 ✉ Main Street (between Hollister and Rose avenues), Santa Monica 🚌 SM1, 8, 10

MARGO LEAVIN GALLERY

www.margoleavingallery.com

Photography, paintings, sculpture and works on paper fill the walls at this cutting-edge art gallery.

➕ G6 ✉ 812 N. Robertson Boulevard, West Hollywood 📞 310/273-0603 🚌 4, 704

MAXFIELD

www.maxfieldla.com

Maxfield stocks designer fashions for men and women, plus lovely furniture, jewelry and housewares.

➕ H5 ✉ 8825 Melrose Avenue, West Hollywood 📞 310/274-8800 🚌 4, 10

MELTDOWN

www.meltcomics.com

This pop-culture shop sells vintage and contemporary comics and

Hollywood and Highland center

collectibles to science-fiction and fantasy fans. The art gallery and special-events space host celebs.
➕ H5 ✉ 7522 W. Sunset Boulevard, Hollywood ☎ 323/851-7223 🚌 217

MISSION STREET
This pretty, tree-shaded street has more than half a dozen antiques dealers, including furniture and collectibles at Mission Antiques (No. 1018); Yoko Japanese Antiques (No. 1011); and linen and bric-a-brac at Hodgson's Antiques (No. 1005).
➕ P4 ✉ Mission Street (between Meridian and Fremont avenues), South Pasadena 🚇 Mission Street

MONTANA AVENUE
www.montanaave.com
Montana Avenue engulfs 10 blocks of super up-scale shopping, designer boutiques, elegant home-decorating emporiums, antique stores and luxurious beauty salons for the woman or man.
➕ D7–C7 ✉ Montana Avenue (between 7th and 17th streets), Santa Monica 🚌 SM3

OLD TOWN PASADENA
Bisected by Colorado Boulevard, this attractively restored enclave has appealing boutiques, galleries and eateries.
➕ P3 ✉ Colorado Boulevard (between Arroyo Parkway and De Lacey Avenue) 🚇 Metro Park 🚌 780; ARTS 10; FT187

PARIS 1900
www.paris1900.com
Paris 1900 carries antique garments and linens, including original Victorian and Edwardian collector's pieces for very special occasions. The store is only open by appointment or chance—so check if your passing.
➕ D8 ✉ 2703 Main Street, Santa Monica ☎ 310/396-0405 🚌 33; SM1, 2, 10

PLASTICA
www.plasticashop.com
The shelves at Plastica are full to the brim with woven bags, chopsticks, teapots, sandals, potato mashers and more—all made from plastic.
➕ H6 ✉ 8405 W. 3rd Street ☎ 323/655-1051 🚌 16

Rodeo Drive

Montana Avenue

THE PUZZLE ZOO

www.puzzlezoo.com

Discover an astounding array of puzzles for beginners to pros, as well as action figures and other endearing toys.

🚩 D8 ✉ 1411 3rd Street Promenade, Santa Monica ☎ 310/393-9201 🚌 4, 704; SM1, 2, 3, 4, 7, 8, 9, 10

RODEO DRIVE

LA's answer to London's Bond Street and Rome's Via Condotti, Rodeo Drive is a gold-plated shopping experience. There are enough top designer clothes and accessories boutiques and chic outdoor malls here to send most credit cards into meltdown.

🚩 F6 ✉ Rodeo Drive (between Santa Monica and Wilshire boulevards), Beverly Hills 🚌 4, 14, 20, 704, 720

ROSE BOWL FLEA MARKET

www.rgcshows.com

Rain or shine, more than 2,500 vendors show up to strike deals over vintage toys and clothes to antique jewelry and rare books. Admission is moderate (the early-bird entry costs more).

🚩 N3 ✉ 1001 Rose Bowl Drive, Pasadena ☎ 323/560-7469 🕐 2nd Sun of month 9–4.30 🚌 ARTS 51, 52

ST. VINCENT JEWELRY CENTER

www.svjc.com

Hundreds of vendors sell their wares here, from platinum and diamonds to inexpensive beads.

🚩 L6 ✉ 650 S. Hill Street ☎ 213/629-2124 🚇 Metro Red Line 🚌 DASH D, E

SAMUEL FRENCH INC

www.samuelfrench.com

For true aficionados, this is the place to find specialist books and essential and obscure film and theater scripts.

🚩 H5 ✉ 7623 Sunset Boulevard, Hollywood ☎ 323/876-0570 🚌 2

SANTA MONICA OUTDOOR ANTIQUE AND COLLECTIBLE MARKET

Hundreds of vendors sell furniture, jewelry, textiles, posters and other vintage delights at ths bimonthly flea market.

🚩 E8 ✉ Santa Monica Airport, Airport Avenue, off S. Bundy Drive ☎ 323/933-2511 🕐 1st Sun of month 8–3, 4th Sun of month 6–3 🚌 SM8

SANTEE ALLEY

www.thesanteealley.com

In the heart of LA's Fashion District, Santee Alley is the place to come for knockoffs of designer shoes and clothing at really low prices. You can pick up fabric and accessories, too. Five times a year, California Market (www.californiamarketcenter.com) has haute designer sales.

🚩 L7 ✉ Between Santee and Maple streets and Olympic Boulevard and 12th Street ☎ 213/746-6776 🕐 Daily 9.30–6 🚌 DASH E

SEVENTH & FIG

This relatively modest open-air Downtown mall has a brace of department stores and a food

SHOP

Take home some designer boots

court; it reopens in fall 2012.
➕ L6 ✉ 735 S. Figueroa Street ☎ 213/955-7150 🚇 7th/Metro 🚌 DASH A, E, F

SMALL WORLD BOOKS
www.smallworldbooks.com
This convenient beachfront emporium sells everything from classics and foreign-language books to beach-holiday mysteries and sex "n" sun sagas.
➕ D9 ✉ 1407 Ocean Front Walk, Venice Beach ☎ 310/399-2360 🚌 33; SM2

SOOLIP PAPERIE & PRESS
www.soolip.com
This amazing stationery shop has racks full of colorful handmade papers, colored inks, hip pens and desk accessories.
➕ H5 ✉ 8646 Melrose Avenue, West Hollywood ☎ 310/360-0545 🚌 4, 10

SOUTH LAKE AVENUE
www.southlakeavenue.org
Pasadena's major shopping area has more than 100 stores.
➕ P3 ✉ Lake Avenue (between California and Colorado boulevards) ☎ 626/792-1259 🚌 485; ARTS 10, 20

SPACE 15 TWENTY
www.space15twenty.com
This self-proclaimed retail experiment features an Urban Outfitters store, plus a rotating selection of designers and artists that the store supports. Musical and artistic performances entertain in the adjacent courtyard.
➕ J5 ✉ 1520 N. Cahuenga Boulevard, Hollywood ☎ 323/465-1893
🚇 Hollywood/Vine 🚌 210

SQUARESVILLE
This barn-like vintage clothing store stocks fashions from decades past for men and women; expect anything from cowboy boots to flower-power hippie dresses and poodle skirts.
➕ K4 ✉ 1800 N. Vermont Avenue, Los Feliz ☎ 323/669-8464 🚌 180, 181

SUNSET PLAZA
Sunset Plaza is an exclusive little cluster of ultrafashionable boutiques and sidewalk bistros on "The Strip."
➕ G5 ✉ Sunset Boulevard (between San Vicente and La Cienega boulevards), West Hollywood 🚌 2

THIRD STREET PROMENADE
www.downtown.com
Shoppers, street musicians and street vendors jostle along the pedestrian-only Promenade with many shopping, dining and entertainment options.
➕ C8, D8 ✉ 3rd Street (between Wilshire Boulevard and Broadway), Santa Monica
🚌 4, 704; SM1, 2, 3, 4, 7, 8, 9, 10

TRINA TURK
www.trinaturk.com
This designers' boutique brings whimsical, colorful Palms Springs

style to women's cocktail and poolside lounge wear in stunning bold prints.
➕ H6 ✉ 3rd 8008 W. 3rd Street, Mid-City ☎ 323/651-1382 🚌 DASH Fairfax, 16, 316

UNIVERSAL CITYWALK
www.citywalkhollywood.com
Get your eclectic gifts and souvenirs from outside Universal Studios Hollywood (▷ 60–61).
➕ H3 ✉ 1000 Universal Center Drive, Universal City ☎ 818/622-4455 🚇 Universal City, then free shuttle bus 🚌 422

VROMAN'S
www.vromansbookstore.com
The oldest bookstore in southern California has a vast selection. There is also a branch selling stationery and gifts down the road at No. 667.
➕ P3 ✉ 695 E. Colorado Boulevard ☎ 626/449-5320 🚌 780; ARTS 10; FT187

WACKO
www.soapplant.com
This part shop, part gallery has wacky items for every taste.
➕ K5 ✉ 4633 Hollywood Boulevard, Hollywood ☎ 323/663-0122 🚌 217

WANNA BUY A WATCH?
www.wannabuyawatch.com
Choose from vintage and contemporary timepieces from Bulova to Betty Boop, Tiffany dress watches and US military issue, plus antique diamond and art-deco jewelry.
➕ H5 ✉ 8465 Melrose Avenue, West Hollywood ☎ 323/653-0467 🚌 4, 10

WASTELAND
www.wastelandclothing.com
Come to Melrose, of course, for vintage clothes for men and women. Last year's designer labels share spaces with 1970s gear, plus shoes, leather and suede.
➕ H5 ✉ 7428 Melrose Avenue, West Hollywood ☎ 323/653-3028 🚌 10

WESTFIELD CENTURY CITY
www.westfield.com/centurycity
This premier outdoor shopping, dining and entertainment complex boasts some 100 stores.
➕ F6 ✉ 10250 Santa Monica Boulevard, Century City ☎ 310/277-3898 🚌 R7, SM7

WESTSIDE PAVILION
www.westsidepavilion.com
Come here for a chic selection of men's and women's fashions, gifts, dining places and movie theaters.
➕ F7 ✉ 10800 W. Pico Boulevard, Century City ☎ 310/474-6255 🚌 R7; SM7

WESTWOOD VILLAGE
www.westwoodvillageonline.com
Students from the neighboring UCLA campus flock to shop at this Mediterranean-style village with movie theaters and music.
➕ E6 ✉ Westwood Boulevard (off Wilshire Boulevard), Westwood 🚌 20, 720; SM1, 2, 3, 8, 11, 12

BEACHWEAR
Having the right bathing suit for the beach is key. Wise shoppers in need follow Angelenos to these destinations: Canyon Beachwear (✉ 106 Entrada Drive, Santa Monica ☎ 310/459-5070); Diane's Beachwear (✉ 620 Wilshire Boulevard, Santa Monica ☎ 310/395-3545); Bikini Beachwear (✉ 705 Montana Avenue, Santa Monica ☎ 310/917-1296); and Beverly Hills Bikini Shop (✉ 245 S. Beverly Drive ☎ 310/550-6331).

Entertainment

Once you've done with sightseeing for the day, you'll find lots of other great things to do with your time in this chapter, even if all you want to do is relax with a drink. In this section establishments are listed alphabetically.

Introduction

In Los Angeles, one of the top entertainment capitals in the world, the hardest part of planning a night on the town is choosing between the many options.

Hollywood and Around

West Hollywood's Sunset Strip has been a perennial favorite for nightclubbers since the city's Golden Era. Visitors and locals alike are bedazzled by such venerable venues as Whisky A Go Go (▷ 137), The Viper Room (▷ 137), the Roxy Theatre (▷ 135) and the Comedy Store (▷ 131), as well as nostalgic bars, hip clubs and Tinseltown's most magnificent cinemas such as Mann's (▷ 34), the vintage Egyptian Theatre (▷ 67–68) and the iconic Cinerama Dome (▷ 131). West Hollywood's Santa Monica Boulevard (aka WeHo) is a hub for LA's gay and lesbian community. Melrose Avenue, further south, and the neighborhoods of Los Feliz and Silverlake, east of Hollywood, attract a young crowd with coffee shops, bars, DJs, comedy and live music clubs.

Santa Monica and the Beaches

In Santa Monica and on the Westside—other good places for a night out—the pedestrian-only Third Street Promenade bustles with open-air cafés, come-as-you-are bars, street musicians and entertainers; the people-watching is some of the best in town. More

PEEK BEHIND THE SCREEN

Only in Los Angeles do you get a chance to be part of the live audience for such a variety of TV shows. Audiences Unlimited (☎ 818/260-0041; www.tvtickets.com) is a major broker of free tickets to studio TV show tapings and occasional awards shows; order tickets online. Or join a behind-the-scenes tour of working TV and movie studios, mostly found in the San Fernando Valley, including the Warner Brothers Studio VIP Tour (▷ 72) and Universal Studios Hollywood (▷ 60–61).

As the sun goes down and the neons are turned on, Los Angeles steps up the pace; lively hotspots include

local watering holes await inland from the beach, including along Main Street heading south toward Venice. By day, Venice's Ocean Front Walk is a carnival of humanity, while after dark bars on Abbot Kinney Boulevard swarm. LA's South Bay coastal towns—especially Manhattan and Hermosa beaches—also have boisterous bars and nightlife scenes.

Downtown LA
In Downtown's cultural corridor, the showpiece Music Center (▷ 134) and Frank Gehry-designed Walt Disney Concert Hall host the city's most acclaimed performing arts groups, including the Los Angeles Philharmonic Orchestra and Los Angeles Opera. The L.A. Live complex (▷ 29) is a major venue for rock concerts at the Nokia Theatre and professional sports at the Staples Center (▷ 136).

West LA
Other venues throughout the city present a range of theatrical works, from classical revivals to innovative, often provocative new works by Southern California playwrights. You may spot well-known talents both on stage and in the audience, especially at theaters here. The UCLA campus is a lively hub for the performing arts, while student-friendly hangouts cluster nearby in Westwood village.

SEEING STARS

Celebrity-spotting is a favorite pastime of Angelenos, who will casually drop into everyday conversations the names of famous folks they've seen around town. No matter where you are, day or night, keep your eyes wide open to see TV and movie stars. Some favorite haunts for celebrity chasers include The Ivy (▷ 144), the Chateau Marmont hotel (▷ 155), Barneys New York department store (▷ 117) in Beverly Hills, Fred Segal boutique (▷ 117), Arclight Cinemas at the Cinerama Dome (▷ 131), and the Malibu Colony Plaza malls in the hideaway of Malibu.

Sunset Boulevard in Hollywood, and Santa Monica, where the Pier lights up the night sky

ENTERTAINMENT

Directory

Beverly Hills to Hollywood

Bars, Pubs and Nightclubs
The Abbey Food and Bar
Avalon Hollywood
Barney's Beanery
Cat & Fiddle Pub
Crown Bar
Dresden Room
Little Temple
Rage
Skybar
Tiki-Ti

Live Music and Performing Arts
The Baked Potato
Comedy Store
Groundlings Theatre & School
Hollywood Bowl
Hotel Cafe
House Of Blues
The Improv
Largo at the Coronet
The Mint
Roxy Theatre
The Troubadour
The Viper Room
Whisky A Go Go

Sports and Leisure
Cinerama Dome
Lucky Strikes Lanes
Samuel Oschin Planetarium
Silent Movie Theatre
Thibiant Beverly Hills

Downtown

Bars, Pubs and Nightclubs
Bordello
Broadway Bar
Golden Gopher
Mayan
Roof Bar at the Standard Downtown

Live Music and Performing Arts
Artani/Japan America Theatre
Music Center

Sports and Leisure
Staples Center

West LA to Malibu

Bars, Pubs and Nightclubs
Bar Chloe
Carbon
Central
Copa d'Oro
The Other Room
The Penthouse
Roosterfish
Whiskey Blue at the W
Ye Olde King's Head

Live Music and Performing Arts
The Actors' Gang
Geffen Playhouse
Harvelle's
Jazz Bakery

McCabe's Guitar Shop
Odyssey Theatre
UCLA Live

Sports and Leisure
Aqua Surf School
Bluewater Sailing
Burke Williams Day Spa
Learn to Surf LA
Malibu Creek State Park
Malibu Surf Shack
Nuart Theatre
Pacific Park
South Bay Bicycle Trail
Will Rogers State Historic Park
Yoga Works

Pasadena

Live Music and Performing Arts
Pasadena Civic Auditorium
Pasadena Symphony

Sports and Leisure
Santa Anita Race Track

Entertainment A-Z

THE ABBEY FOOD AND BAR
www.abbeyfoodandbar.com
This West Hollywood hangout attracts a gay clientele. There's a live DJ most nights and killer martinis.

➕ G5 ✉ 692 N. Robertson Boulevard ☎ 310/289-8410 🚌 4, 704

THE ACTORS' GANG
www.theactorsgang.com
Co-founded by actor Tim Robbins, this small-scale theater revisits classics and promotes new playwrights in an intimate setting.

➕ G7 ✉ 9070 Venice Boulevard, Culver City ☎ 310/838-4264
🚌 3, 733; SM12

AQUA SURF SCHOOL
www.aquasurfschool.com
Aqua Surf offers private lessons, group lessons (Sunday mornings), and package deals. Available year-round, lessons include surfboard, wetsuit and two hours with an instructor.

✉ Various locations ☎ 310/902-7737

ARTANI/JAPAN AMERICA THEATRE
www.jaccc.org
Performances of contemporary and traditional Japanese Noh plays and Kabuki theater are staged here.

➕ L6 ✉ 244 S. San Pedro Street, Little Tokyo ☎ 213/680-3700 🚌 DASH A

AVALON HOLLYWOOD
www.avalonhollywood.com
Formerly the Palace, this renovated

Anyone for cocktails?

club is now sleek and minimalist, with Honey restaurant and a new lounge inside called Bardot.

➕ J5 ✉ 1735 N. Vine Street, Hollywood ☎ 323/462-8900 🚇 Hollywood/Vine
🚌 210, 217, 780

THE BAKED POTATO
www.thebakedpotato.com
This is one of LA's best contemporary jazz spots. The stuffed baked potatoes aren't bad either.

➕ H4 ✉ 3787 Cahuenga Boulevard (at Lankershim), Studio City ☎ 818/980-1615
🚌 156

BAR CHLOE
www.barchloe.com
This intimate hideaway aims for a Parisian salon vibe, serving a mix of classic and specialty cocktails.

➕ D8 ✉ 1449 2nd Street, Santa Monica ☎ 310/899-6999 🕐 Closed Sun 🚌 4, 704; SM1, 7, 8, 10

OPENING TIMES

Most music bars are open nightly from around 9pm until 2am. Headline acts tend to go on after 11pm, when the clubs start to liven up. Nightclubs usually stay open until around 4am, but are typically closed some weeknights (varies by club). Call ahead.

Cocktail bars are two a penny in LA

BARNEY'S BEANERY
www.barneysbeanery.com
This convivial bar has pool tables and a Tex-Mex dining room. There are also outposts in Santa Monica, Pasadena and Westwood.
⊕ G5 ⊠ 8447 Santa Monica Boulevard, West Hollywood ☎ 323/654-2287 🚌 4

BLUEWATER SAILING
www.bluewatersailing.com
There are many options for you at the Pacific Ocean, including chartering your own boat, taking an island cruise or taking a private or group sailing lesson.
⊕ E9 ⊠ 13505 Bali Way, Marina Del Rey ☎ 310/823-5545 (or 866/944-7245 outside California) 🚌 108, SM3

BORDELLO
www.bordellobar.com
Once a legal bordello and the oldest bar Downtown, this spot harkens back to its mischievous roots with a red interior and burlesque nights. There is live music on some nights.
⊕ L6 ⊠ 901 E. 1st Street, Downtown ☎ 213/687-3766 🚌 DASH A, D

BROADWAY BAR
www.broadwaybar.la
It's dark and noisy throughout this nearly 4,000sq ft (370sq m) spot near to the Orpheum. Enjoy the circular bar, the jukebox and the patio (for smokers).
⊕ L7 ⊠ 830 S. Broadway, Downtown ☎ 213/614-9909 🕐 Closed Sun–Mon 🚌 DASH D, E

BURKE WILLIAMS DAY SPA
www.burkewilliamsspa.com
Celebrities come here for hedonistic beauty treatments from facials and pedicures to thermal seaweed wraps and harmony bubble baths.
⊕ D8 ⊠ 1358 4th Street, Santa Monica ☎ 310/587-3366 🚌 4, 704; SM1, 2, 3, 4, 5, 7, 9, 10

CARBON
www.carbonla.com
Carbon draws a young crowd for the nightly DJs spinning an eclectic mix of music; a video streams silent movies. Easy parking.
⊕ G7 ⊠ 9300 Venice Boulevard, Culver City ☎ 310/558-9302 🚌 33, 733; SM12

CAT & FIDDLE PUB
www.thecatandfiddle.com
The outdoor patio, English beer on tap and visiting rock, soul, funk, blues and Latin jazz musicians attract a young crowd.
⊕ H5 ⊠ 6530 Sunset Boulevard, Hollywood ☎ 323/468-3800 🚌 2

CENTRAL
www.centralsapc.com
A Westside club, this unassuming nightspot isn't sleek, but it offers bands that play all types of music, from R&B to rock and alternative.
⊕ D7 ⊠ 1348 14th Street, Santa Monica ☎ 310/451-5040 🚌 4, 704; SM1, 10

CINERAMA DOME

www.arclightcinemas.com

Reserve your seat ahead to view Hollywood blockbusters at this first-class movie theater inside a 1960s geodesic dome. Enjoy an espresso, cocktails, appetizers and the movie-themed gift shop.

J5 ✉ 6360 Sunset Boulevard, Hollywood ☎ 323/464-1478 🚌 2, 210, 302

COMEDY STORE

www.thecomedystore.com

Three stages showcase funsters who are up-and-coming, have made it, or are just plain HUGE at one of the city's premier clubs.

G5 ✉ 8433 Sunset Boulevard, West Hollywood ☎ 323/650-6268 🚌 2

COPA D'ORO

www.copadoro.com

Design-your-own cocktails, while reclining on chic leather couches, during happy hour at Copa d'Oro.

D8 ✉ 217 Broadway, Santa Monica ☎ 310/576-3030 ⏰ Closed Sun 🚌 33; SM1, 2, 7, 8, 10

CROWN BAR

www.crownbarla.com

Sip specialty cocktails with celebrities in a small space with mood lighting, padded walls and shabby-chic mirrors.

H5 ✉ 7321 Santa Monica Boulevard, West Hollywood ☎ 323/882-6774 ⏰ Closed Mon–Thu 🚌 4

DRESDEN ROOM

www.thedresden.com

As seen in the movie *Swingers*, the jazz duo of Marty and Elayne play for a crowd of irony-loving locals in this retro restaurant lounge, usually Tuesday through Saturday nights.

K5 ✉ 760 N. Vermont Avenue, Los Feliz ☎ 323/665-4294 🚌 180, 181

GEFFEN PLAYHOUSE

www.geffenplayhouse.com

This neighborhood theater has a fine reputation, and is intimate enough to host one-person shows.

E6 ✉ 10886 Le Conte Avenue, Westwood ☎ 310/208-5454 🚌 SM1, 2, 3, 8, 11, 12

GOLDEN GOPHER

www.goldengopherbar.com

Get down to this hipster spot with a large patio and arcade games.

L7 ✉ 417 W. 8th Street, Downtown ☎ 213/614-8001 🚌 DASH B, E

GROUNDLINGS THEATRE & SCHOOL

www.groundlings.com

This talented improvizational comedy troupe performs short-run shows; book ahead.

H5 ✉ 7307 Melrose Avenue, West Hollywood ☎ 323/934-4747 🚌 10

HARVELLE'S

www.harvelles.com

Listen to live blues and burlesque at this tiny neighborhood bar.

D8 ✉ 1432 4th Street, Santa Monica ☎ 310/395-1676 🚌 4, 704; SM1, 2, 3, 4, 5, 8, 9, 10

EVENING CAFFEINE

It may seem counter-intuitive to sip coffee at night, but the LA coffeehouse scene is a good alternative to bars and clubs, and many stay open late. Check out worn but cozy Insomnia (✉ 7286 Beverly Boulevard ☎ 323/931-4943), old-timer Bourgeois Pig (✉ 5931 Franklin Avenue ☎ 323/464-6008), or the writer crowd's favorite at Stir Crazy (✉ 6903 Melrose Avenue ☎ 323/934-4656).

HOLLYWOOD BOWL
www.hollywoodbowl.com
A much-loved outdoor summer venue, the Hollywood Bowl hosts the Los Angeles Philharmonic Orchestra, the Hollywood Bowl Orchestra, and other major world music performances.
⊞ H4 ✉ 2301 N. Highland Avenue, Hollywood ☎ 323/850-2000 🚌 156

HOTEL CAFE
www.hotelcafe.com
The quarters are snug at this live-music venue, which also serves sandwiches, salads and espresso drinks.
⊞ J5 ✉ 1623 1/2 N. Cahuenga Boulevard, Hollywood ☎ No phone 🚇 Hollywood/ Vine 🚌 210, 217, 780

HOUSE OF BLUES
www.houseofblues.com
This tin-shack theme restaurant on the Sunset Strip attracts massive crowds and a sprinkling of celebs for Southern food and headline blues-rock acts. There's a gospel brunch on Sunday mornings.
⊞ G5 ✉ 8430 Sunset Boulevard, West Hollywood ☎ 323/848-5100 🚌 2

THE IMPROV
www.improv.com
The Improv is a new-material testing ground for big-name comics. It's best to reserve a table.

⊞ H5 ✉ 8162 Melrose Avenue, West Hollywood ☎ 323/651-2583
🚌 DASH Fairfax, 10

JAZZ BAKERY
www.jazzbakery.com
Formerly housed in Culver City, this liquor-free jazz spot welcomes patrons of all ages. Pastries and hot beverages are served.
✉ Various locations around LA
☎ 310/271-9039

LARGO AT THE CORONET
www.largo-la.com
The beloved Largo took over the old Coronet movie theater space and now accommodates eclectic live performers like Flight of the Conchords and comedian Patton Oswalt. More intimate performances take place in the Little Room bar.
⊞ G5 ✉ 366 N. La Cienega Boulevard, Mid-City ☎ 310/855-0350 🚌 14, 105, 705

LEARN TO SURF LA
www.learntosurfla.com
Year-round surfing lessons are offered by Learn to Surf LA for individuals and groups. Lessons include rental equipment.
✉ Various locations ☎ 310/663-2479

LITTLE TEMPLE
www.littletemple.com
DJs spin hip-hop, Latin salsa, funk,

UNDER STARRY SKIES

In summer, LA's most popular entertainment often takes place outdoors after dark. Concerts at the Hollywood Bowl (▷ 132) and Greek Theatre (✉ 2700 N. Vermont Avenue ☎ 323/665-5857; www.greektheatrela.com) in Griffith Park (▷ 32–33) draw crowds. So does the Twilight Dance Series on Santa Monica Pier (▷ 56), world music and dance shows at Hollywood's family-friendly Ford Amphiteatre (✉ 2580 Cahuenga Boulevard E. ☎ 323/461-3673; www.fordtheatres.org) and Shakespeare's plays at Topanga Canyon (▷ 72). Uniquely, Cinespia (www.cinespia.org) shows movies on an outdoor screen at Hollywood Forever (▷ 68) cemetery.

reggae, nu-soul and world beats on this indie dance floor.

➕ K5 ✉ 4519 Santa Monica Boulevard, Los Feliz ☎ 323/660-4540 🎦 Closed Sun–Mon 🚇 Vermont/Santa Monica 🚌 4

LUCKY STRIKES LANES

www.bowlluckstrike.com

Video screens, DJs and lots of neon add flash to this 12-lane bowling alley in the Hollywood and Highland center. After 7pm, guests must be at least 21.

➕ H5 ✉ 6801 Hollywood Boulevard, Hollywood ☎ 323/467-7776 🚇 Hollywood/Highland 🚌 DASH Hollywood, 12, 780

MALIBU CREEK STATE PARK

www.parks.ca.gov

Once used as a set for *M*A*S*H* and *Planet of the Apes*, this park has 15 miles (24km) of trails shared by bikers, hikers and horseback riders; swimmers and bird-watchers are also welcome.

➕ Off map, west ✉ 1925 Las Virgenes Road, Calabasas ☎ 818/880-0367

MALIBU SURF SHACK

www.malibusurfshack.com

Find surfboards, kayaks, beach chairs and other gear for rent at this shop on the PCH.

➕ Off map, west ✉ 22935 Pacific Coast Highway, Malibu ☎ 310/456-8508

MAYAN

www.clubmayan.com

A fashionably dressy crowd swings to salsa and tropical Latin sounds in this exotic former theater.

➕ L7 ✉ 1038 S. Hill Street, Downtown ☎ 213/746-4674 🎦 Fri–Sat only 🚌 28

MCCABE'S GUITAR SHOP

www.mccabes.com

This guitar shop by day turns into a R&B-rock-jazz-folk showcase on Friday, Saturday and Sunday nights, with some impressive names. It's alcohol-free but tea and cookies are available during musical acts.

➕ E7 ✉ 3101 W. Pico Boulevard, Santa Monica ☎ 310/828-4497 🚌 SM7

THE MINT

www.themintla.com

There's a faithfull crowd at this long-standing small blues, jazz,

Hollywood Bowl

reggae and rock bar with great music and a great atmosphere.
➕ G6 ✉ 6010 W. Pico Boulevard, Mid-City ☎ 323/ 954-9400 🚌 SM5, 7, 13

MUSIC CENTER

www.musiccenter.org
LA's chief performing arts complex includes the Dorothy Chandler Pavilion, the Ahmanson Theatre (musicals, drama and comedy), the Mark Taper Forum (drama and occasional music) and the Frank Gehry-designed Walt Disney Concert Hall (home to the LA Philharmonic's winter season). It is also used by the LA Opera and Los Angeles Master Chorale.
➕ L6 ✉ 135 N. Grand Avenue, Downtown ☎ 213/972-7211 Ⓜ Civic Center 🚌 DASH A, B

NUART THEATRE

www.landmarktheatres.com
This top-notch art house theater shows foreign films, indies, documentaries and more.
➕ E7 ✉ 11272 Santa Monica Boulevard, West LA ☎ 310/281-8223 🚌 4, 704; SM1, 4, 11

ODYSSEY THEATRE

www.odysseytheatre.com
One of the city's most highly regarded avant-garde theater companies offers ensembles and visiting productions.
➕ E7 ✉ 2055 S. Sepulveda Boulevard, West LA ☎ 310/477-2055 🚌 SM4, 5

THE OTHER ROOM

www.theotherroom.com
This wine and beer bar has a great selection of wines by the glass, bottled beer and brews on tap. Don't miss the hip happy hour.
➕ D8 ✉ 1201 Abbot Kinney Boulevard, Venice ☎ 310/396-6230 🚌 SM2

PACIFIC PARK

www.pacpark.com
This seaside fairground offers old-fashioned carnival games and rides for all ages, including a solar-powered Ferris wheel. In summer, twilight dances with world-music bands liven up the pier.
➕ C8 ✉ 380 Santa Monica Pier ☎ 310/260-8744 🕐 Daily, hours vary 🍴 Fast-food stands 💲 Inexpensive per ride 🚌 33, 720; SM1, 4, 7

PASADENA CIVIC AUDITORIUM

www.thepasadenacivic.com
The auditorium is home to a magnificent 1920s Moeller theater organ and various theater, dance and chamber and world music events.
➕ P3 ✉ 300 E. Green Street ☎ 626/449-7360 🚌 181; ARTS 10; FT187

PASADENA SYMPHONY

Pasadena Symphony perform classical music at the Ambassador Auditorium and summer pop concerts by the Rose Bowl.
➕ P3 ✉ 131 S. St. John Avenue, Pasadena ✉ 626/793-7172 🚌 180, 780; ARTS 10

ENTERTAINMENT

THE PENTHOUSE

Swank and a bit of old Hollywood find their way to Santa Monica, with fabulous ocean views from the Huntley Hotel's 18th floor.

➕ C8 ✉ 1111 2nd Street, Santa Monica ☎ 310/393-8080 🚌 20; SM2, 3, 4, 5, 9

RAGE

This packed gay club for boys, serves Top 40, house, Latin and progressive tunes, drag comedy and variety shows.

➕ G5 ✉ 8911 Santa Monica Boulevard, West Hollywood ☎ 310/652-7055 🚌 4, 704

ROOF BAR AT THE STANDARD DOWNTOWN

www.standardhotels.com

This poolside lounge is still the place to be seen, with its white walls, bright accents and tasty bar menu.

➕ 16 ✉ 550 S Flower Street, Downtown ☎ 213/892-8080 🚇 7th St/Metro Center 🚌 DASH A, B, F

ROOSTERFISH

www.roosterfishbar.com

A gay bar that's not in West Hollywood, this laid-back hangout offers a jukebox, pool table and video games.

➕ D9 ✉ 1302 Abbot Kinney Boulevard, Venice ☎ 310/392-2123 🚌 SM2

ROXY THEATRE

www.theroxyonsunset.com

This small, steamy rock venue

showcases major recording acts and new bands via a sound system that will knock your socks off.

➕ G5 ✉ 9009 Sunset Boulevard, West Hollywood ☎ 310/276-2222 or 310/278-9457 🚌 2

SAMUEL OSCHIN PLANETARIUM

www.griffithobservatory.org

Cross the universe in this 285-seat theater, with its fancy projection and sound systems. Tickets are sold day of show only.

➕ J4 ✉ 2800 E. Observatory Road, Griffith Park ☎ 213/ 473-0800 🕐 Shows approximately hourly Wed–Fri 12.45–8.45; Sat–Sun 10.45–8.45 🚌 DASH Weekend Observatory Shuttle

SANTA ANITA RACE TRACK

www.santaanita.com

In the shadow of the San Gabriel Mountains, come here to see thoroughbred horse-racing December 26 to late April, and in October and November. There's free viewing of morning workouts and select weekend tram tours.

➕ S3 ✉ 285 W. Huntington Drive, Arcadia ☎ 626/574-7223 🚌 79; FT187

SILENT MOVIE THEATRE

www.cinefamily.org

It's fitting that the USA's last operational silent movie theater is in this town. Organists offer musical accompaniment for special screening, and filmgoers

JOGGING

LA's most attractive option is probably the 22-mile (35km) South Bay Bicycle Trail (▷ below) running south from Santa Monica. Or try Exposition Park downtown; Griffith Park in the Hollywood Hills; and, just to the west, the great trail around quiet Lake Hollywood reservoir, reached by car off Cahuenga Boulevard.

can also watch classic talkies, too.
➕ H5 ✉ 611 N. Fairfax Avenue, Mid-City
☎ 323/655-2510 🚌 10, 217, 218, 780

SKYBAR

www.mondrianhotel.com
The glamorous Mondrian Hotel (▷ 159) poolside bar has fantastic city views but is only open to hotel guests and those with reservations.
➕ G5 ✉ 8440 Sunset Boulevard, West Hollywood ☎ 323/848-6025 🚌 2

SOUTH BAY BICYCLE TRAIL

www.labikepaths.com
This paved bicycle path starts at Will Rogers State Beach and continues for 22 miles (35km), through Santa Monica and Venice en route to Torrance County Beach. Most of the trail follows alongside the beach, through a few short stretches on city streets. There are a number of spots to rent bikes, rollerblades and other modes of transportation.
➕ Starts at B7

STAPLES CENTER

www.staplescenter.com
This fab sports and entertainment venue is owned by sports and entertainment presenters AEG. This is the home base of the Lakers and Clippers (basketball), Sparks (women's basketball) and Kings (ice hockey) teams.
➕ K7 ✉ 1111 S. Figueroa Street, Downtown ☎ 213/742-7340 🚇 Pico
🚌 DASH F, 81

THIBIANT BEVERLY HILLS

www.thibiantspa.com
A roll-call of Hollywood's most glamorous female movie stars come here for their massages, facials, manicures, makeup and skin treatments.
➕ F6 ✉ 449 N. Cañon Drive, Beverly Hills
☎ 310/278-7565 🚌 4, 14, 16, 704

TIKI-TI

www.tiki-ti.com
Stiff tropical drinks in a bar where smoking is allowed win over Hollywood hipsters. There are normally long lines, but it's worth the wait. Cash only.
➕ K5 ✉ 4427 Sunset Boulevard, Los Feliz
☎ 323/669-9381 🕐 Closed Sun–Tue 🚌 2

THE TROUBADOUR

www.troubadour.com
Doug Weston's venue has staged live premier-league rock and folk music acts since 1957.

SPECTATOR SPORTS

Catch the LA Dodgers (☎ 866/DODGERS) at home at Dodger Stadium, north of Downtown. The LA Lakers (☎ 213/742-7340), the LA Clippers (☎ 888/742-8662) and the LA Kings (☎ 888/546-4752) all play at the Downtown Staples Center (▷ above). The Los Angeles Angels of Anaheim (☎ 714/634-2000) play at Angel Stadium in Orange County. College basketball and football are also very popular, particularly the UCLA Bruins (☎ 310/825-2101) and their crosstown rivals, the USC Trojans (☎ 213/740-4672).

G5 ✉ 9081 Santa Monica Boulevard, West Hollywood ☎ 310/276-6168
🚌 4, 704

UCLA LIVE
www.uclalive
UCLA Live puts on more than 200 music, dance and spoken-word events a year from homegrown and visiting performers.
E6 ✉ UCLA Campus, Westwood
☎ 310/825-2101 🚌 SM1, 2, 3, 8, 11, 12

THE VIPER ROOM
www.viperoom.com
Formerly co-owned by Johnny Depp, the Viper draws cool crowds and big names. The Pussycat Dolls were once the resident band here with their burlesque show.
G5 ✉ 8852 Sunset Boulevard, West Hollywood ☎ 310/358-1881 🚌 2, 202

WHISKEY BLUE AT THE W
www.gerberbars.com
This bar (from Cindy Crawford's husband) exudes an air of pure sophistication with the heat cranked up.
E6 ✉ 930 Hilgard Avenue, Westwood
☎ 310/443-8232 🚌 SM1, 2, 3, 8, 11, 12

WHISKY A GO GO
www.whiskyagogo.com
Though there is less "Go Go" these days, this Sunset Strip stalwart continues to be a haven for hard rockers.
G5 ✉ 8901 Sunset Boulevard, West Hollywood ☎ 310/652-4202 🕐 Closed Sun 🚌 2, 105, 302

WILL ROGERS STATE HISTORIC PARK
wwwparks.ca.gov
There is plenty of space for kids to run wild and picnic on this 186-acre (75ha) hillside ranch, the Western-style home of the "Cowboy Philosopher." There are house tours, a nature trail and horses, stables and occasional polo games to watch.
C6 ✉ 1505 Will Rogers State Park Road (off Sunset Boulevard), Pacific Palisades
☎ 310/454-8212 🕐 Park: daily 8–sunset. House tours: Tue–Fri at 11, 1, 2, Sat–Sun every hour 10–4 🚌 2, 302

YE OLDE KING'S HEAD
www.yeoldekingshead.com
Popular with local Brits, this bar offers draft beer, darts, pub grub and heroic English breakfasts.
D8 ✉ 116 Santa Monica Boulevard, Santa Monica ☎ 310/451-1402 🚌 4, 704; SM1, 2, 7, 8, 10

YOGA WORKS
www.yogaworks.com
Run into your favorite celeb as you assume the cobra pose at this Santa Monica studio. There's also a branch in Westwood.
D7 ✉ 2nd floor, 1426 Montana Avenue, Santa Monica ☎ 310/393-5150 🚌 SM3

A NIGHT AT THE MUSEUMS

Looking for a social scene that's not all about Hollywood clubs? No velvet ropes will stop you from enjoying a night out at the city's biggest and best museums. LACMA (▷ 46–47) hosts free jazz shows many Friday nights. The Natural History Museum of LA County (▷ 52–53) brings in local bands on First Friday nights, when behind-the-scenes tours are offered. On summer Saturday nights, DJs and live bands play at the Getty Center (▷ 24–25). The UCLA Hammer Museum (▷ 58–59) has the coolest calendar of events, from rock bands and performance artists to international festivals and bike nights.

Eat

There are places to eat across the city to suit all tastes and budgets. In this section establishments are listed alphabetically.

EAT

Introduction

Angelenos have a passionate interest in wining and dining—it's no accident that this is where the term "foodie" originated. There are inevitably many places where you would go primarily to see and be seen, but these are still outnumbered by a huge assortment of casual cafés and take-out stalls. And in this most casual of cities, you rarely need to worry about the dress code.

What to Eat

With a diverse population, ethnic cuisine of all kinds is available almost everywhere in LA. The mild climate means fresh produce is abundant, and is incorporated into most menus. There is an exceptionally large choice for vegetarians and the health-conscious.

Where to Eat

Downtown Santa Monica is packed with restaurants and cafés, and there are pricey seafood restaurants along the Pacific Coast Highway. In Beverly Hills you will need a larger budget and to dress up a bit, although the nearby student area of Westwood is less glamorous. The large Hollywood and Highland center has all manner of dining outlets, while trendy restaurants cluster around Melrose Avenue. Downtown has inexpensive ethnic eateries. Pasadena specializes in bistros and cafés.

PRICES AND MEAL TIMES

Except for luxury restaurants, where dinner could easily cost upward of $75 for two people, excluding wine (lunch will be less; typically around $45), dining in LA need not cost an arm and a leg. If you eat in reasonable restaurants, anticipate spending around $8–$12 per person for breakfast, $12–$15 for lunch and $20–$30 for dinner, excluding drinks. Wherever you dine, a tip of 15 to 20 percent of the check is expected. Angelenos generally have lunch between 11.30 and 2, and dinner between 6 and 9, but many restaurants open earlier and close later.

LA eateries range from the simple to the sublime, with something to suit every taste

EL TAQUERO

EAT

Directory

Beverly Hills To Hollywood

Asian
Crustacean
Mr. Chow

Cafés, Delis and Diners
Barney Greengrass
Brighton Coffee Shop
Canter's
Greenblatt's
The Griddle Café
Kokomo
La Brea Bakery
Newsroom Café
Pink's Hot Dogs
Umami Burger
Urth Caffé

California Cuisine
Chaya Brasserie
Larchmont Grill
Lucques
Musso & Frank Grill
Spago Beverly Hills

French
AOC
Comme Ça
Ortolan

Italian
Locanda Veneta
Pizzeria Mozza

Mexican and Southwestern
El Cholo
Mexico City

Miscellaneous
Little Door
Luna Park

Steak and Seafood
The Ivy

Downtown

Asian
Daikokuya
Empress Pavilion
New Moon

Cafés, Delis and Diners
Langer's Deli
Original Pantry Café

Philippe the Original

French
Patina

Mexican and Southwestern
Chichen Itza

Steak and Seafood
Pacific Dining Car
Water Grill

West LA to Malibu

Asian
Katsuya

Cafés, Delis and Diners
Apple Pan
Rose Café
Sidewalk Café

California Cuisine
Chinois
Ford's Filling Station
Michael's

Italian
Valentino
Via Veneto

Mexican and Southwestern
Border Grill

Miscellaneous
Father's Office
Rustic Canyon
Versailles

Steak and Seafood
The Lobster

Pasadena

Asian
Saladang Song
Yujean Kang's

California Cuisine
Parkway Grill
The Raymond

French
Bistro 45

Italian
Mi Piace

Mexican and Southwestern
Mijares

Steak and Seafood
Arroyo Chop House

EAT

Eating A-Z

PRICES

Prices are approximate, based on a 2-course meal for one person.

$$$$	over $50
$$$	$31–$50
$$	$15–$30
$	under $15

AOC $$$

www.aocwinebar.com

This chic wine bar fires up a wood-burning oven and puts a French spin on tapas. It's always crowded.
➕ H6 ✉ 8022 W. 3rd Street, Mid-City ☎ 323/653-6359 🕐 Dinner daily 🚌 DASH Fairfax, 16

APPLE PAN $

Always popular at lunchtime, this LA institution has 1950s counter seating, messy hickory burgers and scrumptious apple and berry pies.
➕ F7 ✉ 10801 W. Pico Boulevard, West LA ☎ 310/475-3585 🕐 Lunch, dinner Tue–Sun 🚌 212

ARROYO CHOP HOUSE $$$$

www.arroyochophouse.com

With its dark wood fittings, this well-established steak house is reminiscent of an old-fashioned club. The chef uses only the best prime beef, or you can have lamb chops or lobster, accompanied by your choice of fresh simply prepared vegetables or salad.
➕ P3 ✉ 536 S. Arroyo Parkway, Pasadena ☎ 626/577-7463 🕐 Dinner daily 🚇 Del Mar 🚌 ARTS 10

BARNEY GREENGRASS $$

The smoked fish, including sturgeon, salmon and cod, is renowned at this chic room atop Barneys New York.
➕ F6 ✉ 9570 Wilshire Boulevard, Beverly Hills ☎ 310/777-5877 🕐 Breakfast, lunch daily 🚌 20, 720

BISTRO 45 $$$

www.bistro45.com

"B45" serves tempting California-French cuisine in a restored art-deco building. The wine list is particularly strong.
➕ P3 ✉ 45 S. Mentor Avenue, Pasadena ☎ 626/795-2478 🕐 Lunch Tue–Fri, dinner Tue–Sun 🚇 Lake 🚌 181; ARTS 10; FT 187

BORDER GRILL $$

www.bordergrill.com

A loud, eclectic crowd flock here for great Mexican food with an inventive twist.
➕ D8 ✉ 1445 4th Street, Santa Monica ☎ 310/451-1655 🕐 Lunch, dinner daily 🚌 4, 704; SM1, 2, 3, 4, 5, 9, 10

BRIGHTON COFFEE SHOP $

This authentic 1930s coffee shop serves sandwich favorites such as grilled cheese, meat loaf and tuna.
➕ F6 ✉ 9600 Brighton Way, Beverly Hills

CALIFORNIA CUISINE

Fresh, seasonal, inventive and health-conscious: These words define California cuisine, the cooking style launched in 1971 by celebrity chef Alice Waters in her lauded Berkeley restaurant, Chez Panisse. The approach caught on throughout the state, with chefs learning to take advantage of seasonal ingredients and appreciate nature's bounty. A fall menu, for example, might include a salad tossed with apples and artisanal blue cheese, butternut squash soup and pumpkin risotto or roast duck with sweet potatoes.

☎ 310/276-7732 🕒 Breakfast, lunch daily 🚌 4, 20, 704, 720

CANTER'S $$

www.cantersdeli.com

This classic Fairfax District deli serves kosher specials, huge pastrami sandwiches, homemade pickles and waitress banter.

➕ H5 ✉ 419 N. Fairfax Avenue, Mid-City ☎ 323/ 651-2030 🚌 14, 217 🕒 Breakfast, lunch, dinner daily

CHAYA BRASSERIE $$$

Chaya is minimalist with a Japanese sensibility that's evident in the innovative and intriguing East-meets-West menu. There's a second location in Venice.

➕ G6 ✉ 8741 Alden Drive, Beverly Hills ☎ 310/859-8833 🕒 Lunch Sun–Fri, dinner daily 🚌 14, 16

CHICHEN ITZA $$

www.chichenitzarestaurant.com

The dishes here spotlight Mexico's Yucatan peninsula, blending Mayan, Spanish and Mexican inside a *mercado* (market).

➕ K8 ✉ 3655 S. Grand Avenue ☎ 213/741-1075 🕒 Breakfast, lunch, dinner daily 🚌 40

CHINOIS $$$$

www.wolfgangpuck.com

Another bustling and stylish showcase for chef Wolfgang Puck's sensational California-Chinese culinary creations.

➕ D8 ✉ 2709 Main Street, Santa Monica ☎ 310/392-9025 🕒 Lunch Wed–Fri, dinner daily 🚌 33, 733; SM1, 8, 10

EL CHOLO $$

www.elcholo.com

This LA institution (established in 1927) serves Mexican fare in hacienda-style surroundings with patio tables for alfresco dining. Other outposts are in Santa Monica and Downtown.

➕ J6 ✉ 1121 S. Western Avenue ☎ 323/ 734-2773 🕒 Lunch, dinner daily 🚌 28, 207, 728

COMME ÇA $$$

www.commecarestaurant.com

This French brasserie in West Hollywood gets a lot of attention for its terrific execution of traditional Parisian fare.

➕ G5 ✉ 8479 Melrose Avenue, West Hollywood ☎ 323/782-1104 🕒 Lunch Mon–Fri, brunch Sat–Sun, dinner daily 🚌 DASH Fairfax, 10

CRUSTACEAN $$$$

www.houseofan.com

The fabulous 1930s Indo-Chinese-style interior here attracts a star-studded clientele to feast on tasty Vietnamese/French cuisine, which features a "secret" menu of family recipes.

➕ F6 ✉ 9646 S. Santa Monica Boulevard, Beverly Hills ☎ 310/205-8990 🕒 Lunch Mon–Fri, dinner daily 🚌 14, 20

A toasted sandwich American-style

EAT

DAIKOKUYA $

www.daikoku-ten.com

Little Tokyo's gold-medal standard for *ramen* (noodle soup) also cooks up succulent pork *gyōza* (dumplings). Expect long lines.

🚉 L6　✉ 327 E. 1st Street, Downtown　☎ 213/626-1680　🕐 Lunch, dinner daily　🚌 DASH B, D

EMPRESS PAVILION $$

www.empresspavilion.com

Huge, busy and ornate, this crowded restaurant is popular for myriad morsels of Hong Kong-style dim sum, and house specials.

🚉 L6　✉ Chinatown Bamboo Plaza, 88 N. Hill Street, Downtown　☎ 213/617-9898　🕐 Breakfast, lunch, dinner daily　🚌 DASH B

FATHER'S OFFICE $$

www.fathersoffice.com

Look for the retro sign outside this jam-packed beer "n" burgers pub that has microbrews on tap and garlicky fries piled high. There's a second location in Culver City.

🚉 C7　✉ 1018 Montana Avenue, Santa Monica　☎ 310/736-2224　🕐 Dinner daily　🚌 SM3

FORD'S FILLING STATION $$$

www.fordsfillingstation.net

Chef-owner Benjamin Ford (son of Harrison) focuses on seasonal ingredients for his New American fare in this loud, industrial space.

🚉 G7　✉ 9531 Culver Boulevard, Culver City　☎ 310/202-1470　🕐 Lunch, dinner daily　🚌 33, 733; SM12

GREENBLATT'S $$

www.greenblattsdeli.com

This haven for homesick New Yorkers serves deli favorites from cheesecake to corned beef.

🚉 G5　✉ 8017 Sunset Boulevard, West Hollywood　☎ 323/656-0606　🕐 Breakfast, lunch, dinner daily　🚌 2

THE GRIDDLE CAFÉ $

www.thegriddlecafe.com

Actors and directors huddle around the diner counter, munching on enormous pancakes with sugary toppings like red velvet and cinnamon crunch. There are omelettes, tacos, burgers and salads, too.

🚉 H5　✉ 7916 Sunset Boulevard, West Hollywood　☎ 323/874-0377　🕐 Breakfast, lunch daily　🚌 2, 302

THE IVY $$$$

Reservations are a must for this celebrity (and paparazzi) hangout. The menu is American comfort food and there's terrace dining.

🚉 G6　✉ 113 N. Robertson Boulevard, Beverly Hills　☎ 310/274-8303　🕐 Lunch, dinner daily　🚌 DASH Fairfax, 14, 220

KATSUYA $$$$

www.sbe.com/katsuya

Philippe Starck designed the ultrastylish Brentwood outpost of this Japanese hot spot that serves creative sushi in a sleek setting.

MIDNIGHT MEALS

Restaurants in LA are not typically open late, but you can find a meal at midnight and into the wee hours. For cheap eats, Pink's Hot Dogs (▷ 148) is open till 2am (until 3am on weekends) and Canter's (▷ 143), a deli on Fairfax Avenue, almost never closes. A bit more upscale is Kate Mantilini (✉ 9101 Wilshire Boulevard ☎ 310/278-3699), which serves American comfort food to an industry crowd until midnight Tue–Thu, 1am Fri–Sat.

There's a sushi bar, of course, and an outdoor terrace.

➕ D6 ✉ 11777 San Vicente Boulevard, Brentwood ☎ 310/207-8744 🕐 Lunch Mon–Fri, dinner daily 🚌 SM3, 4

KOKOMO $–$$
www.kokomo.com
Indulge here on freshly baked muffins, deli sandwiches, steaming bowls of tasty gumbo, salads, burgers and treats like doughnut bread pudding and cupcakes.

➕ H5 ✉ 7385 Beverly Boulevard, Mid-City ☎ 323/933–0773 🕐 Breakfast, lunch daily 🚌 14

LA BREA BAKERY $
www.labreabakery.com
Although this bakery is attached to a terrific Italian restaurant (Campanile), the thing to go for are sourdough sandwiches.

➕ H6 ✉ 624 S. La Brea Avenue, Mid-City 🕐 Breakfast, lunch daily ☎ 323/939-6813 🚌 20, 212, 312, 720

LANGER'S DELI $$
www.langersdeli.com
Langer's is well-known for its hot pastrami sandwiches and other Jewish deli specialties.

➕ K6 ✉ 704 S. Alvarado Street ☎ 213/483-8050 🕐 Breakfast, lunch daily 🚇 Westlake/MacArthur Park 🚌 20, 270

LARCHMONT GRILL $$
www.larchmontgrill.com
Reasonably priced California cuisine is served up in a converted Craftsman-style home; one dining room has a fireplace, while another has views of the Hollywood Hills.

➕ J5 ✉ 5750 Melrose Avenue, Mid-City ☎ 323/464-4277 🕐 Lunch Mon–Fri, dinner Tue–Sun 🚌 10, 210

LITTLE DOOR $$$$
www.thelittledoor.com
The Mediterranean and Moroccan food, served in a romantic atmosphere, includes homemade pita bread, couscous and rack of lamb in a garlic crust. Garden dining is available year-round.

➕ G6 ✉ 8164 W. 3rd Street, Mid-City ☎ 323/951-1210 🕐 Dinner daily 🚌 16, 218

THE LOBSTER $$$–$$$$
www.thelobster.com
Opened in the 1920s, this family seafood restaurant by the Pier rates as highly for its shellfish as its ocean views. Reserve ahead to be sure of a window table.

➕ D8 ✉ 1602 Ocean Street, Santa Monica ☎ 310/458-9294 🕐 Lunch, dinner daily 🚌 33, 733; SM1, 7, 10

LOCANDA VENETA $$$
www.locandaveneta.com
Simple northern Italian cuisine is served in a lively setting at Locanda Veneta. Try sitting in a booth.

➕ H6 ✉ 8638 W. 3rd Street ☎ 310/274-1893 🕐 Lunch Mon–Fri, dinner daily 🚌 DASH Fairfax, 16

EAT

145

Royo y mojo *salad*

LUCQUES $$$$
www.lucques.com
Enjoy the excellent California cuisine served here in an inviting atmosphere. Sunday suppers are a good deal at $45 for a three-course fixed menu.
➕ G5 ✉ 8474 Melrose Avenue, West Hollywood ☎ 323/655-6277 🕐 Lunch Tue–Sat, dinner daily 🚌 4, 10, 704

LUNA PARK $$
www.lunaparkla.com
This popular San Francisco restaurant more than pleases LA diners with its old-fashioned comfort food such as breaded pork cutlets, baby back ribs and s'mores for dessert.
➕ H6 ✉ 672 S. La Brea Avenue, Mid-City ☎ 323/934-2110 🕐 Lunch Mon–Fri, brunch Sat–Sun, dinner daily 🚆 DASH Fairfax, 20, 212, 312, 720

MEXICO CITY $$
www.mexicocityla.com
Los Feliz locals approve of the retro decor, superb enchiladas, Yucatan-style pork and mouth-watering shrimp dishes.
➕ K4 ✉ 2121 Hillhurst Avenue, Los Feliz ☎ 323/661-7227 🕐 Lunch Wed–Sun, dinner daily 🚆 DASH Los Feliz, 180, 181

MICHAEL'S $$$$
www.michaelssantamonica.com
This California culinary pioneer has an impressive contemporary art collection and lovely terrace.
➕ C8 ✉ 1147 3rd Street, Santa Monica ☎ 310/451-0843 🕐 Mon–Fri lunch, Mon–Sat dinner 🚌 20; SM2, 3, 4, 5, 9

MIJARES $$
www.mijaresrestaurant.com
Traditional Mexican fare and famous margaritas have been served here since 1920; expect to wait for a table.
➕ P3 ✉ 145 Palmetto Drive, Pasadena ☎ 626/792-2763 🕐 Lunch Mon–Fri, brunch Sat–Sun, dinner daily 🚇 Fillmore 🚆 ARTS 20

MI PIACE $$$
www.mipiace.com
This popular Italian serves pasta dishes and crispy-crust, New York-style pizzas. The desserts are strong on chocolate.
➕ P3 ✉ 25 E. Colorado Boulevard, Pasadena ☎ 626/795-3131 🕐 Breakfast, lunch, dinner daily 🚇 Memorial Park 🚆 780; ARTS 10; FT187

SUNDAY BRUNCH
When the weekend rolls around, Angelenos gear up to "do" brunch, which is generally served from around 10 or 11 until 2 or 3. Restaurants throughout the city lay on a variation of the combination breakfast and lunch theme with a set-price menu. However, the most popular brunch spots tend to be found on the coast, and patio dining is at a premium.

EAT

MR. CHOW $$$$

www.mrchow.com

Many agents and producers have spent more than 35 years having power lunches at this legendary Chinese restaurant.

🔲 F6 ✉ 344 N. Camden Drive, Beverly Hills ☎ 310/278-9911 🕐 Lunch Mon–Fri, dinner daily 🚌 4, 20, 704, 720

MUSSO & FRANK GRILL $$$

This legendary Hollywood restaurant boasts film-noir flavor, traditional American dishes and perfectly mixed cocktails.

🔲 H5 ✉ 6667 Hollywood Boulevard, Hollywood ☎ 323/467-7788 🕐 Lunch, dinner Tue–Sat 🚇 Hollywood/Highland 🚌 217

NEW MOON $$

www.newmoonrestaurants.com

The Chinese fare here runs the gamut from traditional beef, chicken and noodle dishes to California-influenced plates.

🔲 L7 ✉ 102 W. 9th Street, Downtown ☎ 213/624-0186 🕐 Lunch Mon–Sat 🚌 DASH D

NEWSROOM CAFÉ $$

Come here for the excellent people-watching, along with healthy salads, smoothies and good vegetarian selections.

🔲 G6 ✉ 120 N. Robertson Boulevard, Mid-City ☎ 310/652-4444 🕐 Breakfast, lunch, dinner daily 🚌 14, 220

ORIGINAL PANTRY CAFÉ $

www.pantrycafe.com

Owned by ex-mayor Riordan, this no-nonsense spot serves hearty food on wood tables.

🔲 L6 ✉ 877 S. Figueroa Street, Downtown ☎ 213/972-9279 🕐 Daily 24 hours 🚇 7th/Metro Center 🚌 DASH F

MALLS AND MARKETS

LA's shopping malls, such as the Beverly Center (▷ 115) and the Hollywood and Highland center (▷ 118) are a good source of cheap eats, offering a wide choice of fast-food outlets as well as delis and ethnic take-out counters with shared seating. The down-to-earth Grand Central Market (▷ 30–31) is the best place to find budget bites downtown bar none.

ORTOLAN $$$$

www.ortolanrestaurant.com

One of LA's top chefs serves French food in an elegant but informal setting at this top-flight restaurant. Actress Jeri Ryan is also a partner.

🔲 G6 ✉ 8338 W. 3rd Street, Mid-City ☎ 323/653-3300 🕐 Dinner Tue–Sat 🚌 16, 218

PACIFIC DINING CAR $$$$

www.pacificdiningcar.com

This railroad-theme restaurant offers superb steaks around the clock and a good selection of fish and shellfish. Also in Santa Monica.

🔲 K6 ✉ 1310 W. 6th Street, Downtown ☎ 213/483-6000 🕐 Daily 24 hours 🚌 18

PARKWAY GRILL $$$

www.theparkwaygrill.com

Here you will find cutting-edge California fare with Mediterranean and Asian accents.

🔲 P3 ✉ 510 S. Arroyo Parkway, Pasadena ☎ 626/795-1001 🕐 Lunch Mon–Fri, dinner daily 🚇 Fillmore 🚌 ARTS 20

PATINA $$$$

www.patinarestaurant.com

Patina serves its exceptional modern French cuisine in a posh space adjoining the Walt Disney Concert Hall.

🔲 L6 ✉ 141 S. Grand Avenue, Downtown
☎ 213/972-3331 🕐 Dinner Tue–Sun
🚌 DASH A, B

PHILIPPE THE ORIGINAL $

www.philippes.com

Crusty fried bread, French dip sandwiches piled high, heroic breakfasts and homemade pies will all satisfy your taste buds. Cash only.

🔲 L6 ✉ 1001 N. Alameda Street, Downtown ☎ 213/628-3781 🕐 Breakfast, lunch, dinner daily 🚇 Union Station
🚌 DASH B

PINK'S HOT DOGS $

www.pinkshollywood.com

This take-out stand serves foot-long celebrity-designed hot dogs until 2am (3am Fri and Sat).

🔲 H5 ✉ 709 N. La Brea, Mid-City
☎ 323/931-4223 🚌 10, 212, 312

PIZZERIA MOZZA $$–$$$

www.pizzeriamozza.com

Celeb chefs Mario Batali and Nancy Silverton offer up creative pizzas, antipasti and daily specials. Book in advance.

🔲 H5 ✉ 641 N. Highland Avenue, Mid-City ☎ 323/297-0101 🕐 Lunch, dinner daily 🚌 10

A-MAIZING

Ground corn (*maíz* in Spanish) is a Mexican staple, and the chief ingredient of tortillas, the ubiquitous cornmeal pancakes that turn up in any number of guises on Mexican menus. Some of the most common varieties are soft, folded burritos, baked enchiladas, crescent-shaped, pan-fried quesadillas filled with cheese and chilies and soft or crispy fried and folded tacos (*taco* literally means "snack" in Mexico).

THE RAYMOND $$$

www.theraymond.com

This pretty, historic, California bungalow with patios presents a seasonal, eclectic California menu.

🔲 P4 ✉ 1250 S. Fair Oaks Avenue, Pasadena ☎ 626/441-3136 🕐 Lunch Fri, brunch Sat–Sun, dinner Tue–Sun 🚌 260; ARTS 20

ROSE CAFÉ $

www.rosecafe.com

Outdoor seating, tempting baked food and out-of-work actor/waiters, plus soothing ocean breezes, is what Rose Café is all about.

🔲 D8 ✉ 220 Rose Avenue, Venice
☎ 310/399-0711 🕐 Breakfast, lunch daily
🚌 33; SM1

RUSTIC CANYON $$$

www.rusticcanyonwinebar.com

The Mediterranean-influenced menu is seasonal, but may include handmade pasta, roasted trout and grass-fed beef. There are 20 rotating wines by the glass.

🔲 D7 ✉ 1119 Wilshire Boulevard, Santa Monica ☎ 310/393-7050 🕐 Dinner daily
🚌 20; SM2

SALADANG SONG $$

Artfully presented Thai dishes include a vast assortment of noodle soups, as well as seafood, meat and vegetarian dishes.

🔲 P3 ✉ 363 S. Fair Oaks Avenue, Pasadena ☎ 626/793-5200 🕐 Lunch, dinner daily 🚇 Del Mar 🚌 ARTS 20

SIDEWALK CAFÉ $

www.thesidewalkcafe.com

Enjoy great people-watching from the beachfront terrace, while munching on sandwiches, salads, tostadas and burgers.

🔲 D9 ✉ 1401 Ocean Front Walk, Venice

☎ 310/ 399-5547 ⊙ Breakfast, lunch, dinner daily 🚌 33; SM2

SPAGO BEVERLY HILLS $$$$
www.wolfgangpuck.com
The Beverly Hills outpost of Wolfgang Puck's legendary chain remains the premier place to rub elbows with the rich and famous.
✚ F6 ✉ 176 N. Canon Drive, Beverly Hills ☎ 310/385-0880 ⊙ Lunch Mon–Sat, dinner daily 🚌 14, 20, 720

UMAMI BURGER $
www.umamiburger.com
This smash-hit burger shop with an Asian twist is dedicated to seekers of *umami*, "the fifth taste."
✚ J5 ✉ 1520 N. Cahuenga Boulevard, Hollywood ☎ 323/469-3100 ⊙ Lunch, dinner daily 🚌 210

URTH CAFFÉ $
www.urthcaffe.com
Health-conscious celebrities and artists nosh on wraps, salads and berry bowls at this vegan-friendly café with unique teas and pastries.
✚ G5 ✉ 8565 Melrose Avenue, West Hollywood ☎ 310/659-0628 ⊙ Breakfast, lunch, dinner daily 🚌 DASH Fairfax, 10

VALENTINO $$$$
www.valentinorestaurantgroup.com
Piero Selvaggi serves haute Italian cuisine and an extensive wine list with white-glove service.
✚ E7 ✉ 3115 Pico Boulevard, Santa

Monica ☎ 310/829-4313 ⊙ Lunch Fri, dinner Tue–Sat 🚌 SM7

VERSAILLES $
www.versaillescuban.com
Versailles provides a taste of Havana in Southern California serving family-sized portions at good value.
✚ F7 ✉ 10319 Venice Boulevard, Culver City ☎ 310/558-3168 ⊙ Lunch, dinner daily 🚌 33

VIA VENETO $$$
www.viaveneto.us
This traditional Italian eatery showcases Tuscan and Roman dishes.
✚ D8 ✉ 3009 Main Street, Santa Monica ☎ 310/399-1843 ⊙ Dinner daily 🚌 33; SM1, 10

WATER GRILL $$$
www.watergrill.com
Many flock to this renowned seafood restaurant for the oyster bar.
✚ L6 ✉ 544 S. Grand Avenue, Downtown ☎ 213/891-0900 ⊙ Lunch Mon–Fri, dinner daily 🚌 DASH B

YUJEAN KANG'S $$
www.yujeankangs.com
Chef Yujean Kang creates intriguing Chinese cuisine, with such dishes as tea-smoked duck.
✚ P3 ✉ 67 N. Raymond Avenue, Pasadena ☎ 626/585-0855 ⊙ Lunch, dinner daily 🚇 Memorial Park 🚌 780; ARTS 10; FT187

EAT

CALIFORNIA DRINKING

California wines make a fine accompaniment to almost any meal. Many come from the 450 or so wineries in the Napa and Sonoma valleys north of San Francisco, where common grape varieties include Cabernet Sauvignon and Chardonnay, as well as Californian Zinfandel, genetically identical to Italian Primitivo grapes. Winemakers' names to watch for include, Gundlach-Bundschu, Niebaum-Coppola, Lytton Springs, Ridge, Stags Leap and also *méthode traditionelle* sparkling wines from Domaine Chandon.

Sleep

Ranging from luxurious and modern upmarket hotels to simple budget motels, Los Angeles has accommodations to suit everyone. In this section establishments are listed alphabetically.

SLEEP

Introduction

LA has not only a wide variety of accom-modations, as you would expect from a major city, but also a big choice in where to stay. The city is huge, and is not easily navigable by public transportation.

Location
This is a major consideration when choosing a hotel in a sprawling city like LA. Most hotels listed are on the main east–west transportation corridors between Downtown and the coast at Santa Monica. If you're visiting for more than a few days, consider staying in different areas.

Hotels
Full-service hotels, concentrated in Downtown, Beverly Hills, West LA and Santa Monica, will include amenities such as fitness rooms, indoor pools, laundry service, wireless internet access and valet parking, and this will be reflected in the price. In less fashionable areas, hotels tend to be smaller and less expensive. Most hotels do not include breakfast or parking in their rates, but may allow children to share a room with their parents free of charge if no extra beds are required.

Other Options
Motels are found mainly out of town on the highways; they often have swimming pools and cable TV. Rooms may open directly to the outside so security can be an issue. Some hostels charge as little as $10–$25 per night per person. Bed-and-breakfasts are also popular (▷ panel, 154).

CAMPING

Most campgrounds can be found in Malibu, which offer year-round camping for those who want to rough it. For advance reservations at state parks and beaches in Southern California ☎ 800/444-7275 or visit www.reserveamerica.com online.

From top: A friendly hotel porter on Rodeo Drive; the very exclusive Beverly Hills Hotel; pamper yourself with bathroom treats; beachside hotel, Santa Monica

SLEEP

Directory

Beverly Hills to Hollywood

Budget
Banana Bungalow
   Hollywood Hostel
Beverly Laurel Motor Hotel
Farmer's Daughter
Hollywood Celebrity Hotel
Hollywood Heights Hotel

Mid-Range
Best Western Carlyle Inn
Best Western Sunset
   Plaza Hotel
Four Points LAX
Hollywood Roosevelt Hotel
London West Hollywood
Petit Hermitage
The Standard

Luxury
Beverly Hills Hotel
Beverly Wilshire
Chateau Marmont
Hotel Bel-Air
Mondrian
Peninsula Beverly Hills

Downtown

Mid-Range
Figueroa Hotel
Hilton Checkers Hotel
Kyoto Grand Hotel
Millennium Biltmore
   Hotel Los Angeles

West LA to Mailbu

Budget
Hostelling International
   Santa Monica
The Inn at Venice Beach
Sea Shore Motel

Mid-Range
Channel Road Inn
   Bed and Breakfast
Embassy Hotel Apartments
Georgian Hotel
Hotel Angeleno

Luxury
Casa Del Mar
Shutters on the Beach

Pasadena

Luxury
The Langham Huntington
   Hotel & Spa

Further Afield

Budget
Best Western Stovall's Inn

Mid-Range
The Belamar Hotel
Holiday Inn & Suites Anaheim

SLEEP

Sleeping A-Z

BANANA BUNGALOW HOLLYWOOD HOSTEL $

www.bananabungalow.com

This longtime favorite has rooms and dorms, a friendly international atmosphere, free airport pickup, movie lounge with satellite TV, laundry and kitchen, free parking and wireless internet. No curfew.

➕ H5 ✉ 603 N. Fairfax Avenue, Mid-City ☎ 877/666-2002 🍴 Restaurants nearby 🚌 DASH Fairfax, 10, 217, 780

THE BELAMAR HOTEL $$

www.thebelamar.com

Near LAX, this non-smoking hotel has 127 guest rooms and suites, though none with ocean views. Rooms have flat-screen TVs and sumptuous linens. Outside is a heated pool and garden.

➕ Off map, south ✉ 3501 Sepulveda Boulevard, Manhattan Beach ☎ 310/750-0300 🍴 Restaurant 🚌 232

BEST WESTERN CARLYLE INN $$

www.carlyle-inn.com

This delightful 32-room hotel

offers a spa, fitness center, free local shuttle and complimentary breakfast buffet.

➕ G6 ✉ 1119 S. Robertson Boulevard, West LA ☎ 310/275-4445 or 800/322-7595 🚌 220; SM5, 7

BEST WESTERN STOVALL'S INN $

www.stovallshotels.com

Close to Disneyland, this large hotel with 290 rooms and two swimming pools is always mobbed with kids. There are free shuttles to Disneyland.

➕ Off map, southeast ✉ 1110 W. Katella Avenue, Anaheim ☎ 714/778-1880 or 800/854-8177 🍴 Breakfast included 🚌 460

BEST WESTERN SUNSET PLAZA HOTEL $$

www.sunsetplazahotel.com

This may not be the city's most glamorous hotel, but the location right on Sunset Strip is hard to beat. The 100 rooms are spacious.

➕ G5 ✉ 8400 Sunset Boulevard, West Hollywood ☎ 323/654-0750 or 800/421-3652 🍴 Breakfast included 🚌 2, 302

BEVERLY HILLS HOTEL $$$

www.beverlyhillshotel.com

The 210 rooms and 23 VIP bungalows at this legendary pink palace, where celebs hide out, are set on a 12-acre (5ha) landscaped and palm-fringed site.

➕ F5 ✉ 9641 Sunset Boulevard, Beverly

SLEEP

Hills ☎ 310/276-2251 or 800/650-1842
🍴 Restaurant, coffee shop, poolside
café 🚗 2, 302

BEVERLY LAUREL MOTOR HOTEL $

In a terrific location near Melrose Avenue and Museum Row, some of the 52 rooms here have kitchens.
🔢 G6 ✉ 8018 Beverly Boulevard, Mid-City ☎ 323/651-2441 🚗 14

BEVERLY WILSHIRE $$$

www.fourseasons.com
This sumptuous European-style hotel has 386 luxury rooms and suites and a full-service spa.
🔢 F6 ✉ 9500 Wilshire Boulevard, Beverly Hills ☎ 310/275-5200 or 800/819-5053 🍴 Excellent restaurant from Wolfgang Puck 🚗 20, 720

CASA DEL MAR $$$

www.hotelcasadelmar.com
Located right on the beach, this "roaring twenties" seaside hotel has 129 renovated guest rooms, most with views of the Pacific. Amenities include flat-screen TVs in the bathroom and a spa.
🔢 D8 ✉ 1910 Ocean Way, Santa Monica ☎ 310/581-5533 or 800/898-6999 🍴 Restaurant, lounge 🚗 33; SM1, 7, 10

CHANNEL ROAD INN BED AND BREAKFAST $$

www.channelroadinn.com
In Santa Monica Canyon, this original 1910 Colonial Revival house is crammed with period antiques. The 15 individual rooms have private baths. Bicycles, a library and hot tub are available. Tea and cookies are laid on each afternoon, with wine and cheese served in the evenings.

🔢 C7 ✉ 219 W. Channel Road, Santa Monica ☎ 310/459-1920 🍴 Breakfast included 🚗 9

CHATEAU MARMONT $$$

www.chateaumarmont.com
This castle-style 1927 building, with over 60 rooms plus bungalows and cottages, was a favorite of Gable, Lombard and Harlow et al. John Belushi died here.
🔢 G5 ✉ 8221 Sunset Boulevard, West Hollywood ☎ 323/656-1010 or 800/242-8328 🍴 Dining room with fine wine cellar 🚗 2, 302

EMBASSY HOTEL APARTMENTS $$

www.embassyhotelapts.com
Near the ocean and Third Street Promenade, these Mediterranean-style apartments, built in 1927,

Beverly Wiltshire hotel

SLEEP

offer numerous studio and bedroom suites with kitchens. Single rooms are also available.
🏠 C7 ✉ 1001 Third Street, Santa Monica
☎ 310/394-1279 🚌 20, 720; SM4

FARMER'S DAUGHTER $

www.farmersdaughterhotel.com
Across the street from the farmers' market, this is a friendly family-owned budget option. You get a good deal for your money. There are 66 rooms, a pool and an on-site restaurant called Tart.
🏠 H6 ✉ 115 S. Fairfax Avenue, Mid-City
☎ 323/937-3930 or 800/334-1658
🚌 DASH Fairfax, 14, 16, 217

FIGUEROA HOTEL $$

www.figueroahotel.com
This useful central business, Moroccan-themed hotel was built in 1925 with 285 airy rooms.
🏠 L6 ✉ 939 S. Figueroa Street, Downtown ☎ 213/ 627-8971 or 800/ 421-9092 🍴 Restaurant 🚌 DASH F

FOUR POINTS LAX $$

www.fourpointslax.com
A free airport pickup is available at this comfortable airport hotel with 573 high-rise rooms.
🏠 Off map, south ✉ 9750 Airport Boulevard ☎ 310/645-4600 or 800/ 368-7764 🍴 Restaurant

GEORGIAN HOTEL $$

www.georgianhotel.com
Two blocks from Santa Monica

Pier, this oceanfront art-deco hotel is a historic gem from 1933. Some of the 84 petite, earth-tone rooms and suites enjoy ocean views.
🏠 C8 ✉ 415 Ocean Avenue, Santa Monica
☎ 310/395-9945 or 800/538-8147
🍴 Restaurant 🚌 4, 20, 33, 720, 733; SM1, 7, 8, 10

HILTON CHECKERS HOTEL $$

www.hiltoncheckers.com
This elegant hotel is a good option for visitors searching for 4-star luxury in Downtown. There's a rooftop swimming pool and spa.
🏠 L6 ✉ 535 S. Grand Avenue, Downtown
☎ 213/624-0000 or 800/445-8667
🍴 Restaurant 🚇 Pershing Square
🚌 DASH B

HOLIDAY INN & SUITES ANAHEIM $$

www.hianaheim.com
Impeccably tidy, this family-friendly high-rise hotel with 255 rooms is just a block from Disneyland.
🏠 Off map, southeast ✉ 1240 S. Walnut Street, Anaheim ☎ 714/535-0300 or 800/308-5312 🍴 Restaurant 🚌 460

HOLLYWOOD CELEBRITY HOTEL $

www.hotelcelebrity.com
No-fuss hotel rooms and apartment suites with kitchens are uphill from the Hollywood and Highland center. Free parking.
🏠 H5 ✉ 1775 Orchid Avenue, Hollywood

MAGIC ACT

When traveling with children, the Magic Castle Hotel (✉ 7025 Franklin Avenue, Hollywood ☎ 323/851-0800 or 0800/741-4915; www.magiccastle.com), a 40-unit option in Hollywood, has a unique offering: professional tricksters. Adults have access to the private Magic Castle Club in the evenings, while families can see the magic show at brunch on weekends. Rooms and suites come equipped with full kitchens; continental breakfast is included.

SLEEP

Spoil yourself at the Hotel Bel-Air

☎ 323/850-6464 or 800/222-7017
🍴 Breakfast included 🚇 Hollywood/Highland

HOLLYWOOD HEIGHTS HOTEL $
www.hollywoodheightshotel.com
A heated swimming pool and gym feature at this converted high-rise with 160 modern rooms. Some pets are accepted (fee $75).
✚ H5 ✉ 2005 N. Highland Avenue, Hollywood ☎ 323/876-8600 or 866/696-3157 🍴 Restaurant 🚇 Hollywood/Highland 🚌 156

HOLLYWOOD ROOSEVELT HOTEL $$
www.hollywoodroosevelt.com
This refurbished Hollywood legend has some poolside cabana rooms among the 300 units.
✚ H5 ✉ 7000 Hollywood Boulevard, Hollywood ☎ 323/466-7000 or 800/950-7667 🍴 Restaurants 🚇 Hollywood/Highland 🚌 DASH Hollywood, 217

HOSTELLING INTERNATIONAL SANTA MONICA $
www.hilosangeles.org
Close to the Santa Monica Pier, this good-size hostel (260 beds) has a courtyard, laundry, library, tours and activities. Some private rooms are available.
✚ D8 ✉ 1436 2nd Street, Santa Monica ☎ 310/393-9913 or 888/464-4872 🚌 4, 20; SM1, 7, 8, 10

HOTEL ANGELENO $$
www.hotelangeleno.com
Near the Getty Center (▷ 24–25), this chic mid-20th-century circular icon is conveniently just off the freeway. An outdoor heated pool, fireplace and a penthouse lounge with city views are perks.
✚ D6 ✉ 170 N. Church Lane, Brentwood ☎ 310/598-7859 or 888/796-4671 🍴 Restaurant, lounge 🚌 2, 302; SM14

HOTEL BEL-AIR $$$
www.hotelbelair.com
LA's most romantic hotel, with its signature pink-stucco Spanish Colonial style, is tucked away in a wooded canyon. The 106 rooms have recently been refurbished.
✚ E5 ✉ 701 Stone Canyon Road, Bel-Air ☎ 310/472-1211 or 800/648-4097 🍴 Restaurant

THE INN AT VENICE BEACH $

www.innatvenicebeach.com

This colorful multistory motel close to Venice's boardwalk has 43 tidy rooms; those facing the street can be noisy.

➕ E9 ✉ 327 Washington Boulevard, Venice ☎ 310/821-2557 or 800/828-0688 🍴 Restaurants nearby; breakfast included 🚌 33

KYOTO GRAND HOTEL $$

www.kyotograndhotel.com

This contemporary high-rise building in Little Tokyo is close to Union Station. The rooms are plain but perfectly comfortable, and there's a restful Japanese garden and spa.

➕ L6 ✉ 120 S. Los Angeles Street, Downtown ☎ 213/629-1200 or 888/354-0831 🍴 Restaurant 🚌 DASH A, D

THE LANGHAM HUNTINGTON HOTEL & SPA $$$

www.langhamhotels.com

Beautifully restored, this 1907 hotel features 380 rooms and suites, deluxe facilities and stunning gardens.

➕ P4 ✉ 1401 S. Oak Knoll Avenue, Pasadena ☎ 626/568-3900 or 800/588-9141 🍴 Excellent restaurant and Sun brunch

LONDON WEST HOLLYWOOD $$

www.thelondonwesthollywood.com

This 200-suite hotel has a rooftop pool and a restaurant from English celeb chef Gordon Ramsay. There is also a fitness center.

➕ G5 ✉ 1020 N. San Vicente Boulevard, West Hollywood ☎ 866/282-4560 🍴 Excellent restaurant 🚌 2, 4, 105, 305

MILLENNIUM BILTMORE HOTEL LOS ANGELES $$

www.millenniumhotels.com

A national historic landmark, the Biltmore opened in 1923 and has many famous associations. It was once home to the Academy Awards and birthplace of the Oscars; JFK accepted the Democratic presidential nomination here in 1960. The rooms themselves may be unexciting, but the grandeur of the public areas and the thoughtful service more

Relax on the balcony at Shutters on the Beach, Santa Monica

than compensate for this.

➕ L6 ✉ 506 S. Grand Avenue, Downtown ☎ 213/ 624-1011 or 800/245-8673 🍴 Restaurants ◉ Pershing Square 🚌 DASH B

MONDRIAN $$$

www.mondrianhotel.com

Edgy and postmodern, this party-central hotel bang on the Sunset Strip has 237 large rooms with floor-to-ceiling windows, city views and bamboo floors.

➕ G5 ✉ 8440 Sunset Boulevard, West Hollywood ☎ 323/650-8999 or 800/697-1791 🍴 Restaurant 🚌 2, 105, 302

PENINSULA BEVERLY HILLS $$$

www.beverlyhills.peninsula.com

This ultrachic hideaway for celebrities, with discreet and personalized service, has 194 splendid rooms conveniently near the poshest shopping streets.

➕ F6 ✉ 9882 S. Santa Monica Boulevard, Beverly Hills ☎ 310/551-2888 or 800/462-7899 🍴 Belvedere Restaurant 🚌 4, 20, 704, 720

PETIT HERMITAGE $$

www.lepetitwesthollywood.com

In the residential district of Melrose Place, equidistant from Beverly Hills and Hollywood, this classy hotel has 79 luxurious boutique suites with fireplaces, and a rooftop garden swimming pool.

➕ G5 ✉ 8822 Cynthia Street, West

Hollywood ☎ 310/854-1114 or 800/835-7997 🍴 Restaurant 🚌 4, 704

SEA SHORE MOTEL $

www.seashoremotel.com

This retro two-story motel is an affordable budget choice near the beach, shopping and art galleries. All 20 basic rooms are clean and comfortable and the suites have kitchens.

➕ D8 ✉ 2637 Main Street, Santa Monica ☎ 310/392-2787 🍴 Cafés nearby 🚌 33, 733; SM1, 10

SHUTTERS ON THE BEACH $$$

www.shuttersonthebeach.com

Created by Malibu and White House interior designer Michael Smith, the 198 New England beach cottage-style rooms here are a short walk from the sea. Ask about surfing lessons, bicycle rentals and yoga classes on the sand.

➕ D8 ✉ One Pico Boulevard, Santa Monica ☎ 310/458-0030 or 800/334-9000 🍴 Very good restaurant, One Pico 🚌 33; SM1, 7, 10

THE STANDARD $$

www.standardhotels.com

Tongue-in-cheek design and a hip, youthful crowd define this rock "n" roll crash pad on the Sunset Strip. The 139 fashionably mod rooms are sized up to extra large.

➕ G5 ✉ 8300 Sunset Boulevard, West Hollywood ☎ 323/650-9090 🍴 24-hour restaurant 🚌 2, 302

SLEEP

Need to Know

This section takes you through all the practical aspects of your trip to make it run more smoothly and to give you confidence before you go and while you are there.

NEED TO KNOW

Planning Ahead

WHEN TO GO

Los Angeles is mild and temperate, with sun-shine and fair weather pretty much guaranteed from May to October. Humidity ranges from 65 to 79 percent. Spring, early summer and early fall are the best times to visit; crowds aren't too big and the weather should be perfect. Beware of cloudy coastal skies from May to July, usually in the mornings—Angelenos call this June gloom.

TIME

Los Angeles is on Pacific Standard Time (US West Coast); 3 hours behind New York, 8 hours behind the UK.

TEMPERATURE

JAN	FEB	MAR	APR	MAY	JUN	JUL	AUG	SEP	OCT	NOV	DEC
66°F	67°F	69°F	71°F	73°F	77°F	82°F	83°F	82°F	78°F	73°F	67°F
19°C	19°C	21°C	22°C	23°C	25°C	28°C	28°C	28°C	26°C	23°C	19°C

Spring (mid-March to late June) is usually dry and comfortable.

Summer (late June to mid-September) is perfect beach and theme-park weather. Late summer can be smoggy, though humidity is usually low.

Fall (mid-September to November) is fair to warm. Days are gorgeous, nights crisp.

Winter (December to mid-March) brings warm days interspersed with cool and even freezing nights. Sweaters and jackets are usually necessary after dark.

WHAT'S ON

January *Rose Parade*: Pasadena's New Year's Day spectacular accompanying the Rose Bowl college football game.

January/February *Chinese New Year*: The Golden Dragon Parade winds through Chinatown.

February *Academy Awards*: Celebrities hit Hollywood.

March *LA Marathon and Bike Tour*: 3-mile (5km) running race and bicycle event.

April *Songkran Festival (Thai New Year)*: Huge street fair in East Hollywood.

Doo Dah Parade: Pasadena's Rose Parade with its own brand of eccentricity.

May *Cinco de Mayo*: Mexico's independence day (May 5), liveliest on Downtown's Olvera Street.

June *Playboy Jazz Festival*: Hollywood Bowl.

LA Pride: LGBTQ parade and festival in West Hollywood.

June–September *Hollywood Bowl Summer Series*: Evening open-air concerts.

July *Lotus Festival*: Asian and Pacific Islander cultural festivities at Echo Park Lake.

August *Nisei Week*: Japanese-American cultural heritage event.

September *Los Angeles Birthday Celebrations*: Celebrates the founding of the city (Sep 4).

LA County Fair: LA County Fairplex Fairgrounds, Pomona.

October *Alpine Village Oktoberfest*: In Torrance.

November *Día de los Muertos*: Olvera Street celebrates the Day of the Dead (Nov 1).

December *Griffith Park Holiday Light Festival*: Month-long spectacular light display.

Las Posadas: Illuminated processions on Downtown's Olvera Street.

LOS ANGELES ONLINE

www.lacvb.com
The Los Angeles Convention and Visitors Bureau covers cultural attractions, suggested itineraries, city statistics and general travel information. The site also has useful links.

www.losangeles.citysearch.com
You'll get loads of interesting information: the top celebrity hangouts, chic shops, new movies, hot pubs and a range of picks from the best spa to the tastiest burrito.

www.latimes.com
The daily *Los Angeles Times* has national and local news, and sections devoted to entertainment, food, sports, politics, health, southern California living, travel and business.

www.latimes.com/entertainment
This section of the *Los Angeles Times* gives a comprehensive overview of current films, theater, exhibits, lectures, concerts, sports and other entertainment happenings in and around the city. Reviewers also give input.

www.lamag.com
The online version of the slick monthly *Los Angeles Magazine* is a great guide to restaurants, museums, nightclubs, outdoor events, concerts, art galleries and fashion boutiques.

www.laweekly.com
This alternative weekly tabloid provides loads of information about the city, covering live music, nightclubs, dining, performing arts, shopping, special events, local news, politics and lots more.

www.lacity.org
The official website of the City of Los Angeles provides tourist and recreational information, as well as a detailed introduction to the city.

www.lawa.org
This is the official website for Los Angeles World Airports.

USEFUL TRAVEL SITES

www.theAA.com
A great resource for the essentials, ranging from destination information to travel insurance policies. There is also a UK facility for ordering travel guides and maps online.

www.fodors.com
A complete travel-planning site. You can research prices and weather; book air tickets, cars and rooms; ask questions (and get answers) from fellow travelers; and find links to other sites.

INTERNET CAFÉS

FedEx Office
Branches throughout the LA area offer internet access and business services. Prices vary, but internet access is about 20–30¢ per minute.

➕ L6 ✉ 800 Wilshire Boulevard, Downtown
☎ 213/892-1700
🕓 Mon–Fri 7am–11pm, Sat–Sun 9–9

➕ J5 ✉ 1440 Vine Street, Hollywood ☎ 323/871-1300
🕓 Mon–Fri 7am–11pm, Sat–Sun 9–9

➕ G5 ✉ 8471 Beverly Boulevard, Mid-City
☎ 323/782-6905
🕓 Mon–Fri 7am–11pm, Sat–Sun 9–9

Getting There

ENTRY REQUIREMENTS

Visitors to the US must show a full passport, valid for at least six months and will need to complete an Electronic System of Travel Authorization (ESTA™) before traveling. ESTA™ is a web-based system and can only be accessed online. For more information, and to complete the ESTA™ form, visit https://esta.cbp.dhs.gov. Most UK citizens and visitors from other countries belonging to the Visa Waiver Program can enter without a visa, but you must have a return or onward ticket. Regulations do change, so always check before you travel with the US Embassy ☎ 020 7499 9000; www.usembassy.org.uk. Leave plenty of time to clear security as levels of checks are constantly being stepped up.

CUSTOMS

● Visitors from outside the US, aged 21 or over, may import duty-free: 200 cigarettes or 50 non-Cuban cigars or 4.4lb (2kg) of tobacco; 2 pints (1L) of liquor; and gifts up to $100 in value.

● Restricted import items include meat, seeds, plants and fruit.

● Some medication bought over the counter abroad may be prescription-only in the US and may be confiscated. Bring a doctor's certificate for essential medication.

AIRPORTS

Los Angeles International Airport (LAX) is a 17-mile (27km) drive southwest of Downtown. It is served by all major domestic carriers and many international airlines. The flight from London takes around 10 hours; from New York 6 hours.

FROM LOS ANGELES INTERNATIONAL AIRPORT

For airport information tel 310/646-5252. Car rental companies, airport area hotels and private off-airport parking lots provide free shuttles that pick up from the ground transportation island outside the lower level baggage claim areas.

Door-to-door, 24-hour shuttle bus and shared-ride van services to all areas of the city, such as SuperShuttle (tel 800/782-6600 or 800/258-3826; www.supershuttle.com) and Prime Time Shuttle (tel 310/536-7922 or 800/733-8267), also depart from the ground transportation island. The journey to Downtown takes around 30–60 minutes, depending on traffic, and costs $15–$18.

The airport provides free, frequent shuttle buses between all eight terminals (Shuttle A), and the remote parking lots (Shuttle C). Shuttle C also stops at the Metro Bus Center terminal for bus connections into the city and around the county ($1.85–$3.35). Shuttle G serves the Metro Green Line Aviation Station.

LAX FlyAway express buses to downtown LA (one-way $7) and Westwood (one-way $5) leave from the upper departures level outside each airport terminal. For Disneyland,

Gray Line (tel 714/978-8855 or 800/828-6699; www.grayline.com) offers a direct coach service every 30–60 minutes between LAX and Anaheim resort hotels costing $20–$35 and taking 60–90 minutes.

A cab to Downtown or Hollywood costs between $45 and $60 and takes 30–70 minutes, depending on traffic.

LAX BY DESIGN
The control tower at the Los Angeles International Airport was created by local architect Kate Diamond, whose 1995 design evokes a stylized palm tree. It makes a fine counterpoint to the nearby Theme Building, the spidery structure that has long been the symbol of LAX and contains the space fantasy restaurant and bar called Encounter.

ARRIVING BY AIR: OUTSIDE LOS ANGELES
If you are flying in from other states or cities in the US, you may arrive at one of the region's many smaller airports, which include Bob Hope Airport, formerly Burbank Airport (tel 818/840-8840; www.burbankairport.com) in Burbank; John Wayne Airport (tel 949/252-5200; www.ocair.com) Santa Ana, Orange County; Long Beach Airport (tel 562/570-2600; www.lgb.org); or Ontario International Airport in Ontario (tel 909/937 2700; www.lawa.org), convenient only if you are headed first to the desert.

ARRIVING BY BUS
LA's main Greyhound terminal is Downtown (1716 E. 7th Street). There are also terminals in Anaheim, Hollywood and Long Beach. For more information tel 800/231-2222; www.greyhound.com.

ARRIVING BY TRAIN
Visitors and commuters arrive at Union Station (800 N. Alameda Street), just north of Downtown, on the Metro Red Line and DASH shuttle bus routes. For Amtrak information tel 800/872-7245; www.amtrak.com.

INSURANCE
● Domestic travelers should check their policies and ensure they are covered against loss and theft as well as medical emergencies.
● For non-US citizens, it is vital that travel insurance covers medical expenses in addition to accidents, trip cancellation, baggage loss and theft. Check the policy covers any continuing treatment for a chronic condition.

VISITORS WITH DISABILITIES
Visitors with disabilities should have few troubles navigating LA, one of the world's leaders in assuring an accessible environment. All public buildings are wheelchair accessible. In addition, many attractions, hotels and restaurants offer access. Most street corners have sloped curbs, and city buses are fitted with automatic wheelchair lifts, handgrips and designated seating areas. For more information contact the Los Angeles Convention and Visitors Bureau (☎ 213/689-8822; www.discoverlosangeles.com/planning-your-trip/travelresources/) or LA County Infoline (☎ 211 or 800/339-6993).

Getting Around

THE METRO (MTA)

www.metro.net

☎ 511 or 323/GOMETRO

The Los Angeles County Metropolitan Transit Authority (MTA) runs the Metro buses and rail lines and provides the most extensive coverage of the city, although many lines have a reduced evening and weekend service.

● Major bus routes run roughly every 15 minutes, with a reduced service at night.

● The Metro system has 180 Metro Bus lines and 8 Metro Rail lines, covering about 80 miles (129km), but they are only of limited use when trying to get from one part of the city to another.

● A single journey by bus or rail is $1.50, while the Metro Day Pass, which gives unlimited use of all Metro bus and rail lines for a day, costs $6. You can buy it at any Metro station or on board any Metro Bus.

● A single ticket is only valid on one line. If you change lines, you must buy another ticket.

● There is a small additional fee of 35¢ for transferring to a municipal bus, referred to as Metro-to-Muni Transfer.

● There are no gates to pass through or conductors to collect tickets, but MTA does carry out random ticket inspections.

BUSES

Buses operated by the Los Angeles County Metropolitan Transit Authority (MTA or Metro; www.metro.net) provide the most extensive coverage of the city, but many lines have a reduced evening and weekend service.

DASH shuttle buses, operated by the Los Angeles Department of Transportation, (tel 213/808-2273; www.ladottransit.com/dash, cost 35¢) serve various neighborhoods throughout the city, but primarily Downtown LA. Most DASH routes run every 5–30 minutes from 7am to 5pm weekdays, with limited (or no) service on weekends.

Big Blue Bus routes (SM tel 310/454-5444; www.bigbluebus.com, cost $1) run throughout Santa Monica, connecting to Venice Beach, Culver City, Westwood, Brentwood and other West LA neighborhoods. Most routes operate daily from around 7am until 8pm or later.

Other municipal bus lines include Pasadena's Foothill Transit (FT tel 626/931-7210; www.foothilltransit.org) and Area Rapid Transit System (ARTS tel 626/398-8973; ww2.cityofpasadena.net/trans/transit/); and the South Bay's Beach Cities Transit (BCT tel 866/263-8444; www.redondo.org).

Have correct change ready for the machine on boarding. Fares are based on the number of zones traveled and certain express services cost more.

METRO RAIL LINE

● The Red Line subway extends from Union Station across Downtown and northwest to Los Feliz, Hollywood and Universal City in 25 minutes.

● The Blue Line runs above ground from Downtown to Long Beach; about 55 minutes.

● The Gold Line goes from Union Station northeast to Pasadena in 25 minutes.

● The Green Line goes toward South Beaches and passes near the airport, but is otherwise of little interest to tourists.

● The Purple Line shares six stations with the Red Line and continues to mid-Wilshire.

• Opened in late 2011, the Expo Line goes south from Downtown to Expo Park/USC.

TAXIS

It is virtually impossible to hail a cab in the street, except possibly Downtown. Hotels and transport terminals are good places to find a cab, and restaurants will order one for you at the end of your evening. Useful taxi company dispatchers are: Checker Cab (tel 213/482-3456 or 800/300-5007 or Independent Cab (tel 213/385-8294 or 800/521-8294).

DRIVING

LA is a sprawling city not that well served by public transportation, so it's a good idea to rent a car at the airport to get around. Seatbelts are required and children under six must be secured in a safety or booster seat. As everyone else is also driving, traffic snarls (jams) are an almost constant hazard. These are useful routes from LAX:
• To reach Marina del Rey, Venice, Santa Monica and Malibu, follow the signs to Sepulveda Boulevard north, then leave Sepulveda to take Lincoln Boulevard (here serving as Highway 1) to head north.
• For West LA and Beverly Hills, follow signs to Century Freeway (I-05) or take Century Boulevard east to the San Diego Freeway (I-405). Head north on I-405 till you cross Santa Monica Freeway (I-10), then exit on Santa Monica, Wilshire or Sunset boulevards.
• For Hollywood, take I-105 east to I-405 north to I-10 east to Hwy 110 north (toward Pasadena), then take the Hollywood Freeway (Hwy 101) north. Alternatively, take I-405 north to I-10 east and get off at La Cienega, Fairfax or La Brea and head north to West Hollywood or Hollywood.
• For Downtown LA, take Century Freeway (I-105) east to Harbor Freeway (I-110) north toward Pasadena, passing Downtown LA exits.
• To reach Pasadena, follow the directions for Downtown LA above, but continue north on Hwy 110 (called the Pasadena Freeway north of Downtown LA).

RULES OF THE ROAD

• It is legal to turn right on a red light unless otherwise posted.
• Pedestrians have right of way at crosswalks.
• At four-way crossings without traffic lights, the law decrees that cars cross in order of arrival at the intersection; if two cars arrive simultaneously, the car to the right has priority. In reality, the driver who dares wins.
• Freeway carpool lanes can be used by any car carrying the requisite number of passengers (generally two or three), indicated by signs posted on the freeway.
• Unless otherwise posted, the speed limit is 55 or 65mph (88 or 104kph) on urban freeways, 35mph (56kph) on major thorough-fares, 25mph (40kph) on residential and other streets.

GUIDED TOURS IN LA

Los Angeles Conservancy
☎ 213/430-4219;
www.laconservancy.org.
Themed historical walking tours.
Starline Tours
☎ 800/959-3131;
www.starlinetours.com.
Tours of Hollywood and the stars homes.
American Limousines
☎ 877/885-4667;
www.americanlimos.org
Gondola Getaway
☎ 562/433-9595;
www.gondolagetaaways.com

Essential Facts

MONEY

The unit of currency is the dollar (=100 cents). Notes (bills) come in denominations of $1, $5, $10, $20, $50 and $100; coins come in 25¢ (a quarter), 10¢ (a dime), 5¢ (a nickel) and 1¢ (a penny).

ELECTRICITY

In the USA electricity runs on 110/120V, 50/60Hz. Socket plugs have two flat vertical prongs, sometimes with an additional third rounded prong for grounding. Most overseas visitors will need a converter to plug in computer laptops, travel gadgets, etc.

PUBLIC HOLIDAYS

● New Year's Day: January 1
● Martin Luther King, Jr. Day: third Monday of January
● Presidents' Day: third Monday of February
● Memorial Day: last Monday in May
● Independence Day: July 4
● Labor Day: first Monday in September
● Columbus Day: second Monday in October
● Veterans' Day: November 11
● Thanksgiving Day: fourth Thursday in November
● Christmas Day: December 25

CONSULATES

● Australia: Century Plaza Towers, 2029 Century Park East, Suite 3150, tel 310/229-4800
● Canada: 550 S. Hope Street, 9th Floor, tel 213/346-2700
● Germany: 6222 Wilshire Boulevard, Suite 500, tel 323/930-2703
● Netherlands: 11766 Wilshire Boulevard, tel 310/268-1598
● New Zealand: 2425 Olympic Boulevard, Santa Monica, tel 310/566-6555
● UK: 11766 Wilshire Boulevard, Suite 1200, tel 310/481-0031

ETIQUETTE

● LA dress is generally casual. Men rarely don jacket or tie to dine in even the smartest restaurants.
● Smoking is illegal in all public buildings, and is now banned in bars and restaurants as well. It is permitted in outdoor seating areas of restaurants, though do not expect your neighbors to be friendly about it. There are designated smoking rooms in some hotels.
● Tipping: 15–20 percent is expected by waiters; 15 percent for cab drivers; $2 per bag for porters; $2–$5 per night for hotel maids; 15–20 percent for hairdressers; and $2–$5 is usual for valet parking.

LIQUOR LAWS

● Bars can open at any time between 6am and 2am, though most don't open before 11am and close by midnight (later on Friday and Saturday). Licensed restaurants can serve liquor throughout their hours of business except between 2am and 6am. To buy or consume liquor in California, you must be 21 or older. Expect to be asked for ID.

LOST AND FOUND

● LA International Airport: Contact your airline and ask for its lost-and-found department or call LAX Airport Police (tel 310/417-0440).
● MTA (Metro Buses and Metro Rail) Lost & Found (tel 323/937-8920)

MAIL AND TELEPHONES

● Post offices are generally open Mon–Fri 8.30 or 9am to 5pm; Sat until noon or 1pm.

● Local calls made from a payphone cost 35–50¢.

● LA has a number of local telephone codes. Some calls within the LA area require more than a 35–50¢ deposit. Dial the number and a recorded operator message gives the minimum deposit.

● The area code for Downtown Los Angeles is 213. Other area codes that could be useful include 323 (the area immediately surrounding Downtown and Hollywood); 310 (Beverly Hills, West LA, Santa Monica, Venice); 562 (Long Beach and other South Bay cities); 626 (Pasadena); 818 (San Fernando Valley).

● Many businesses have free phone numbers, prefixed 800, 888, 877 and 866. First dial "1" (i.e. "1-800").

● To call the US from the UK dial 001. To call the UK from the US dial 011 44, then drop the first "0" from the area code.

MEDICAL TREATMENT

● Many hotels can arrange for referrals to a local doctor or dentist. Or look under "Physicians and Surgeons" or "Dentists" in the *Yellow Pages*.

● Most city hospitals accept emergency cases. Those with well-equipped 24-hour emergency rooms include:
Cedars-Sinai Medical Center (8700 Beverly Boulevard, Mid-City, tel 310/423-3277) and Good Samaritan Hospital (1225 Wilshire Boulevard, Downtown, tel 213/977-2121).

MEDICINES

● Visitors from outside the US using medication regularly will find that although many familiar drugs are available (probably under unfamiliar names), it is preferable to bring a supply.

● If you intend to buy prescription drugs in the US, you will need to bring a covering note from your doctor.

POPULATION

According to the US Census Bureau, the population of Los Angeles County in 2010 was 9,818,605, up 3.1 percent since 2000. There are nearly 2,420 persons per square mile.

OPENING HOURS

● Most businesses and government offices are open 9am to 5pm from Monday to Friday; some banks may keep later hours and also open 9am to 1pm on Saturday.

● Shop hours are 10am to 6pm from Monday to Saturday, noon to 5pm on Sunday; shopping malls and centers close later. Some supermarkets, pharmacies, convenience stores and gas stations are open 24 hours.

● Restaurants are usually open for breakfast from 7am until 10am, lunch from 11.30am to 2pm and dinner from 5.30pm to 9pm (10pm on Friday and Saturday).

● Many bars are open 4pm to 11pm daily (later on weekends); some open as early as 11am.

● Nightclubs are typically open from 10pm to 4am (closed some weeknights).

NEED TO KNOW

VISITOR INFORMATION

● **Los Angeles Convention and Visitors Bureau**
✉ 333 S. Hope Street, 18th Floor, Los Angeles, CA 90071
☎ 213/689-8822

● **LA Visitor Information Centers:**

Downtown
✉ 685 S. Figueroa Street (between Wilshire and 7th Street), Los Angeles, CA 90017 ☎ 213/689-8822
🕒 Mon–Fri 8.30–5

Hollywood
✉ Hollywood and Highland Center ☎ 323/467-6412
🕒 Mon–Sat 10–10, Sun 10–7

● **Pasadena Convention & Visitors Bureau**
✉ 300 E. Green Street, Pasadena, CA 91101
☎ 626/795-9311 or 800/307-7977 🕒 Mon–Fri 8–5, Sat 10–4

● **Santa Monica Convention & Visitors Bureau**
✉ 1920 Main Street, Suite B, Santa Monica, CA 90401
☎ 310/393-7593 or 800/544-5319 🕒 Daily 9–5.30

Visitor Information Kiosk
✉ 1400 Ocean Avenue, Palisades Park ☎ 310/393-0410 🕒 Daily 10–4 (9–5 Jun–Aug)

MONEY MATTERS
● Nearly all banks have ATMs.
● Credit cards, a secure alternative to cash, are widely accepted.
● US dollar traveler's checks function like cash in all but small shops and eateries; $20 and $50 denominations are most useful.
● A 9.75 percent sales tax is added to all retail prices.

NEWSPAPERS AND MAGAZINES
● LA's English-language daily newspapers are the *Los Angeles Times* (local and international news) and the *Los Angeles Daily News*.
● The free *LA Weekly* has excellent events and entertainment listings.

SENIOR CITIZENS
● Senior citizens discounts are available on a number of services as well as admission to attractions. Take proof of age.
● Inquire ahead for discounts when making reservations for hotels and car rentals.
● Casual restaurants may offer senior citizens discounts on certain menus, and early-bird specials provide savings.

SENSIBLE PRECAUTIONS
● Few visitors ever see LA's high-crime areas, the South-Central district and East LA.
● Venice Beach is unpleasant after dark, infested with drunks and drug peddlers.
● Don't carry easily snatched bags or cameras.
● Carry only as much cash as you require.
● Don't leave anything of value in cars, even when it is hidden.
● Most hotels provide a safe for valuables.
● Report lost or stolen items to the nearest police precinct if you plan to make a claim.

STUDENT TRAVELERS
● Students with appropriate ID may be entitled to reduced admission to attractions.
● Anyone under 21 may not be allowed into nightclubs.
● To rent a car in California, you typically must be aged 25 or older.

Books and Films

LA loves telling stories about itself, whether on the printed page or the silver screen. From Hollywood and beyond, this city is a hotbed of literary and celluloid creativity.

Hollywood Noir

Ever since Hollywood began making movies in the early 20th century, screenwriters have lined up to supply storylines. Even some famous American novelists worked on studio lots, including F. Scott Fitzgerald. The acknowledged master of the hardboiled crime novel genre was Raymond Chandler, whose fictional detective Phillip Marlowe chased bad guys and dames around pseudonymous LA neighborhoods. Most of Chandler's pulp fiction novels were adapted into Hollywood hits, such as *The Big Sleep* (1946), starring Humphrey Bogart. Today, the hardboiled crime-writing tradition is carried on by authors like Walter Mosley—*Devil in a Blue Dress* (1990), later a film starring Denzel Washington; and James Ellroy—*L.A. Confidential* (1990), which also became an Academy Award-winning movie.

Celluloid Classics

Countless thousands of movies have been made here since Cecil B. DeMille directed Hollywood's first feature film, *The Squaw Man* (1914). In some of Hollywood's most enduring classics, it turns the camera on itself. Roman Polanski's *Chinatown* (1974), starring Jack Nicholson and Faye Dunaway, is a gripping tale of greed, corruption and crime in 1930s LA. Comedian Steve Martin's pop-culture *LA Story* (1991) is a hilarious look at the everyday eccentricities of Southern California life. *Singin' in the Rain* (1952), a musical starring Gene Kelly and Debbie Reynolds, celebrates movie magic, while *Sunset Boulevard* (1950), directed by Billy Wilder, and *A Star Is Born* (1937, 1945 and 1976), examine the darker sides of Hollywood stardom. More modern movies that have already become classics set in LA include Robert Altman's sardonic *The Player* (1992) and Quentin Tarantino's *Pulp Fiction* (1994).

CULTURAL CRITICS

Starting in the counter-cultural 1960s, novelists and filmmakers began casting a critical eye over LA's cultural landscape. Charles Bukowski wrote *Post Office* (1971) about the sordid side of life and work Downtown. *Los Angeles Times* reporter Richard Vasquez defended the rights of Mexican immigrants and narrated their struggles for justice in his novel *Chicano* (1970). Parodying the mindless consumerism of the 1980s, Brett Easton Ellis' novel *Less Than Zero* (1985) depicted the drug-addled, sex-crazed lives of Beverly Hills college kids, while John Singleton's hard-hitting film *Boyz in the Hood* (1991) examined gang violence in South Central LA.

Index

The Automobile Association would like to thank the following photographers, companies and picture libraries for their assistance in the preparation of this book.

Abbreviations for the picture credits are as follows – (t) top; (b) bottom; (c) center; (l) left; (r) right; (AA) AA World Travel Library.

This book makes reference to various Disney copyrighted characters, trademarks, marks and registered marks owned by The Walt Disney Company and Disney Enterprises, Inc.

Every effort has been made to trace the copyright holders, and we apologise in advance for any unintentional omissions or errors. We would be pleased to apply any corrections in a following edition of this publication.

Los Angeles' 25 Best

WRITTEN BY Emma Stanford
ADDITIONAL WRITING BY Sara Benson
SERIES EDITOR Marie-Claire Jefferies
REVIEWING EDITOR Linda Schmidt
PROJECT EDITOR Apostrophe S Ltd
COVER DESIGN Guido Caroti
DESIGN WORK Lesley Mitchell
INDEXER Joanne Phillips
IMAGE RETOUCHING AND REPRO Sarah Montgomery

ISBN 978-0-307-92810-8

SEVENTH EDITION

IMPORTANT TIP
Time inevitably brings changes, so always confirm prices, travel facts, and other perishable information when it matters. Although Fodor's cannot accept responsibility for errors, you can use this guide in the confidence that we have taken every care to ensure its accuracy.

SPECIAL SALES
This book is available for special discounts for bulk purchases for sales promotions or premiums. Special editions, including personalized covers, excerpts of existing books, and corporate imprints, can be created in large quantities for special needs. For more information, write to Special Markets/Premium Sales, 1745 Broadway, 3-2, New York, NY 10019 or email specialmarkets@randomhouse.com.

Color separation by AA Digital Department
Printed and bound by Leo Paper Products, China

10 9 8 7 6 5 4 3 2 1

Cover image: zxvisual/iStockphoto

A05120
Maps in this title produced from map data © Tele Atlas N.V. 2007
Transport map © Communicarta Ltd, UK

Tele Atlas

Titles in the Series